All the Beautiful Things

Beth Doherty

All the Beautiful Things

Finding Truth, Beauty and Goodness in a Fractured Church

Beth Doherty

Adelaide
2020

Text copyright © Beth Doherty for all papers in this collection. All rights reserved. Except for any fair dealing permitted under the Copyright Act, no part of this book may be reproduced by any means without prior permission. Inquiries should be made to the publisher.

Cover design: Myf Cadwallader
Photograph: Beth Doherty
Layout by Extel Solutions
Text: Minion Pro size 10 &11

ISBN: 978-1-925612-88-2   soft
       978-1-925612-89-9   hard
       978-1-925612-90-5   epub
       978-1-925612-91-2   pdf

Published by:

An imprint of the ATF Press Publishing
Group owned by ATF (Australia) Ltd.
PO Box 504
Hindmarsh, SA 5007
ABN 90 116 359 963
www.atfpress.com
Making a lasting impact

'Cultivate with love the seeds of goodness, beauty and truth that God sows in every new generation.'

    Pope Francis

Table of Contents

1. Beauty from Ashes — 1
2. Of Saints and Sinners — 23
3. The Gift of the Sacraments — 31
4. The Name of God Is Mercy — 41
5. Women Who Follow Jesus — 49
6. Education in the Catholic Tradition — 57
7. The Parish Community — 65
8. Celebrating Christmas and Easter — 73
9. Worshipping in Spirit and Truth — 83
10. Let Justice Roll Down — 93
11. Rebuilding, Renewal, Reform — 103
12. Jesus, Yesterday, Today and Tomorrow — 119
13. Epilogue — 123
14. References — 131

Chapter One
Beauty from Ashes

'The beauty of the Catholic Church is that it has a sacramental structure that can hold its own with the best out of any tradition. It has a mystical system and content that can hold its own with the best out of Tibet . . . it's an amazing tradition, but I think you need to be critical.'[1]

There are few passages of scripture that more aptly describe the story of Christianity than Isaiah 61:3:

To provide for those who mourn in Zion—
    to give them a garland instead of ashes,
the oil of gladness instead of mourning,
    the mantle of praise instead of a faint spirit.
They will be called oaks of righteousness,
    the planting of the Lord, to display his glory.

A garland instead of ashes . . . The oil of gladness . . . A mantle of praise.

The story, that is the story of Christianity, and of life itself is still being written on our hearts.

For those who cling on to belief, however haphazardly, there lives the possibility that from suffering and sadness, from the ashes of destruction, can come great beauty.

Beauty from ashes is about redemption. It's about a cross. It's about gathering together threads, grains, broken glass, shreds, fragments and dust, and transforming them.

---

1. John O'Donohue, *Beauty: The Invisible Embrace* (New York: Harper Collins Publishers, 2004).

It is about building up something new from the ruins of our lives. It is about the transformative power of God's liberating love to make beautiful things out of brokenness.

It's about an apparently illegitimate child born in a stable, surrounded by oxen and sheep, a humble saviour born into poverty and turmoil.

'I saw the angel in the marble', said the great Renaissance sculptor and painter Michelangelo, 'and I carved until I set him free.'

November, 2017.
The gentle scent of flowers, incense and candles, an odour pregnant with meaning, greets me as I enter the side door of the cathedral.

I bless myself, kissing my hand quickly after making the sign of the cross, a gesture I learned in Latin America and that reminds me of a faith that has carried me from before I was born.

There is a lot of propaganda in this church. As the mother church of the archdiocese, it's only natural that it would, at times, become a repository for the good, the bad and the crazy.

There are magazines and leaflets, there are Catholic newspapers from around the country, miraculous medals with printed instructions on how to pray the rosary, and flyers espousing different interest groups' positions on the latest political battles.

Some of the material is comforting, beautifully designed and crafted with exquisite prose, written objectively and thoughtfully. Some of it is less so, provoking a range of emotions, some of them rage, division and exclusion.

And so it is with this faith.

The Catholic Church is nothing if not an institution that invites and gives a home to all the paradoxes of life.

People's opinions, cultures, preferences and political leanings, economic status, race and language, all somehow fit and co-exist under this banner we call Catholicism.

Indeed, how is it that Catholicism manages to maintain a fragile unity, even across every nation and tribe?

On this day, I am struck by the smells that greet me. I notice them, because they remind me of that unusual mix of incense and roses and of candles just extinguished.

The smell is beautiful, it's the scent of prayer.

It causes me to wonder why it is, at age thirty-six, when most of my peers have chosen to leave, or simply put aside, this tradition, that I still find solace, beauty and truth in my Catholicism.

Sometimes, I think the reason I am still here is because of some misguided sense of obligation.

Week in, week out, I still attend.

It's not always the same parish mind you. I'm itinerant like many of my generation.

One week will be in a cathedral complete with ornate vestments, and choral sounds coming from the choir loft; the following week could be in a suburban church with colourful banners on the wall and dove-shaped cut-outs made by primary school children preparing for the sacraments.

This means that my experience of parish as a connecting community is limited, and this isn't always helpful.

My wondering about Catholicism's enduring pull for me led me to wonder what others thought.

So, I set out to survey some people using social media.

My questions included: Why do you go to mass? (if at all), and what do you find beautiful about Catholicism in this time and place?

Have the scandals in the Church affected your feelings about your own faith?

I asked people to give honest opinions about their experiences of parish and the sacraments, their thoughts on church teaching, and on the place of women in leadership.

I asked them not to hide from the things they find difficult, particularly in the light of recent scandals.

The questions were deliberately varied, and the responses reflected a wide array of opinions and backgrounds.

One thing I found almost unanimously was a hunger for change.

Very few were happy with the status quo.

Many were bewildered, concerned, angry, and thirsting, hungering for reform. Some had been working at the fringes of the Church for years.

Some had given up hope.

The percentage who felt that the tradition should, for the most part, stay as it is was less than two per cent.

One particularly insightful response came from a member of my immediate family, my brother, Dr Bernard Doherty. He is a historian, a revert to the Catholic faith after a brief stint in the Greek Orthodox church and has many years of education across a wide range of Protestant faculties. He wrote:

> Despite its many flaws the Catholic Church maintains the fullest and most compelling expression of the Christian faith. Catholicism embodies a direct historical and enduring sacramental link back to the early Christian tradition and while developing organically has continued to proclaim that inheritance.
>
> While other Christians are no less Christian, I have found by rich experience of the diversity of other Christian traditions that only Catholicism has drawn to itself the sufficient cumulative spiritual resources to fully express that in a holistic way in the face of unbelief . . .
>
> Catholicism is as cultural as it is religious, in a way that is far more inextricable than most other Christian creeds. It is woven into the warp and woof of life in a way far more difficult to untangle than other forms of Christianity. One rarely encounters someone who says they're a lapsed Baptist, for instance, implying that they still maintain, if only tentatively, some vestiges of self-identification with that tradition. In contrast, one frequently meets 'lapsed Catholics' who, while often embittered toward the Church, cannot bring themselves to entirely disown their inheritance.

Another thoughtful response was the following:

> The tradition. Knowing that hundreds of thousands of people before me have participated in the exact same thing; knowing that, at the same time, there are Catholic masses being held all throughout the world in various languages and countries; knowing that, because the tradition has been alive for so long, I can find countless pieces of evidence and writing supporting it and maybe even questioning it to make it stronger. All these things are beautiful to me.

Others had similar things to say, expressed in a variety of ways. Some were quick responses, dashed off between feeding young children, others were the considered views of academics, tradespeople, teachers, journalists, lawyers, priests and religious; others were midnight rants over a glass of wine, and others again were casual interviews over tea or something stronger.

> *The Church is where I am sustained in my commitment to Christ and his mission. It has transformed my life and has been the force that powers any good that I do. At its best it is a place of beauty and truth.*

Before I started writing this book, I had been thinking about beauty a lot.

The first time I heard the quote 'the world will be saved by beauty' was while reading Kate Hennessy's biography of the famed twentieth century servant of God (and Kate's grandmother), Dorothy Day.

The quote comes originally from the pen of Dostoevsky in the novel *The Idiot*. The main character of this novel is Prince Myshkin, depicted as a Christ-figure:

> *Out of the mouth of this idiot comes a clearer vision of beauty and reality than those around him, his clarity heightened even in the midst of his sickness.*[2]

Pope John Paul II quoted the same line from Dostoevsky in his *Letter to Artists*, under the heading 'The saving power of beauty'. He wrote:

> *People of today and tomorrow need this enthusiasm [of wonder] if they are to meet and master the crucial challenges which stand before us. Thanks to this enthusiasm, humanity, every time it loses its way, will be able to lift itself up and set out again on the right path. In this sense it has been said with profound insight that 'beauty will save the world'.*[3]

So, where do we find beauty, saving beauty? Can beauty save the Church, or will ugliness, brokenness and evil triumph?

---

2. Quoted and discussed further in R Jared Staudt, 'Beauty Will Save the World: From the Mouth of an Idiot to the Pen of a Pope', in *Crisis Magazine*, 10 July 2013 at <http://www.crisismagazine.com/2013/beauty-will-save-the-world-from-the-mouth-of-an-idiot-to-the-pen-of-a-pope>. Accessed 9 September 2019.
3. Pope John Paul II, *Letter of His Holiness Pope John Paul II to Artists* at <https://w2.vatican.va/content/john-paul-ii/en/letters/1999/documents/hf_jp-ii_let_23041999_artists.html>. Accessed 9 September 2019.

Purveyors of beauty—artists, craftspeople, designers, architects, musicians, actors, media, marketing and advertising professionals—have us convinced of a plethora of ways we might find beauty, depending on the time, fashions and cultural influencers.

But could it be that baptism with holy water in the name of the carpenter from Nazareth, that weekly or even daily nourishment from his body and blood might be the beauty we seek?

Could it be that the smells of incense accompanied by a grand processional and a blessing, or an anointing with oil, may be the healing balm our hungry, broken souls need?

Might it be that pondering the words of scripture in our hearts might give us a living encounter with Christ?

Might it be that in serving bread to the poor and questioning the structures that keep them in poverty we will be brought face to face with Christ, as Mother Teresa put it, in the 'distressing disguise of the poor'?

Could it be that these things form together into something quite beautiful in which we might find our deepest longings met?

Belonging is a crucial part of this question. None of the above is possible without community. As one survey respondent wrote when asked about why they remain in the Church:

> *Because the Church holds all my life and does it in community—life, death, joy, sorrow, struggle, failure, success, hope. It has provided me with a unique foundation that gives me resilience and strength. The sports club and the pub are both great but I get something in Catholic community I can't get there in the same way. The faith community I'm part of supports and affirms me. The Eucharist unites us all in solidarity with those whose bodies are broken and their blood poured out around the world. At the same time, it is a meal in sacred community and is my key to mission.*
>
> *Some people in the Church can be hard to deal with, and some are the best people I have ever met. Saints and sinners together. I remember my mum and dad and their love of God that flowed naturally into mission. I stood beside them at Mass every week. We talked about all people being welcomed and invited to the table. We invited people to our home table who needed family. I 'remember' them every time I take the bread, drink the cup, speak the words and sing the songs. The Mass and the community are powerful sources of love for me. It sustains me and helps me grow.*

Quite reasonably, you might ask if it is right, or even possible, to say today that beauty can be found in Church or faith?

Practice of Catholicism has decreased at an alarming rate over the last century, in no small part due to scandals that have plagued the Church throughout its history, and which more recently have dominated any headline referring to this institution.

The second largest 'denomination' of people in the United States are ex-Catholics, according to Brandon Vogt in his book *Why I Am Catholic (and You Should Be Too)*.[4]

Only one sixth of the numbers who leave the Church join it.

The abuse crisis, or crises, more than any other single issue is making people throughout the world question the very credibility of this institution. So why would we buy into it?

Chiaroscuro is defined as 'the treatment of light and shade in drawing and painting', and it is a good concept to describe the experience of being part of the Church today.

It's not a word I hear often, but it stood out to me one day when I saw it on Twitter.

Using social media as a communication form, some Church leaders can be surprisingly pithy and often insightful, even in 280 characters or less.

Reflecting in a tweet in mid-December 2017, an Australian archbishop wrote *what he was experiencing at the time.*

> Reflecting on joy with thousands of young people at #ACYF17 (Australian Catholic Youth Festival) and awaiting the joyless final report of the Royal Commission . . . the mind-boggling chiaroscuro of the Church.[5]

In these words, Archbishop Coleridge enunciated something I'd been trying to put my finger on.

A human church will necessarily reflect its human members, in all their light and shade.

---

4. Brandon Vogt, *Why I Am Catholic (and You Should Be Too)* (Notre Dame, Ind: Ave Maria Press, 2017), 3.
5. @Archbishop Mark (Mark Coleridge), 8 December 2017, 5:31pm at <https://twitter.com/ArchbishopMark/status/939019500422230016>. Accessed 8 December 2017.

There is no perfect political party, workplace or sporting team, so why should there be a perfect church?

Although we may believe and hold dear that Catholicism is divinely inspired, being a human institution, it will always have some measure of light and shadow.

Indeed, I have not a few times asked myself: by being Catholic, am I defending the indefensible?

For many of the survey respondents who shared their views, there was a sense of 'where else would I go', re-capturing the words of the disciple Peter who asked Jesus: 'Lord, to whom shall we go?' (Jn 6:68).

> *Because where else would I go? I made a commitment as an adult to this faith—the faith promoted by this Church. The Church is full of sinners. We need to recognise this and be heartened that Jesus came for sinners, meaning, the weak, the broken, the unsure. When we put people in the Church on a pedestal, we are setting ourselves up for disappointment. We are all the body of Christ.*

And yet, being part of the body of Christ means being a part of a broken body.

It's being part of a continuum.

Often, maybe even mostly, it means Good Friday instead of Easter Sunday.

Sometimes it means a sorrow that lasts, and a waiting for the joy that comes with the morning.

I remember a late-night phone call from an abuse survivor when I worked in media relations for the Australian bishops.

He asked me how I could live with myself, putting my name at the bottom of media releases and, by doing so, seeming to defend the Church.

It was a fair question, one that I ask again and again, and which has prompted me to enter the journey of this book. In truth, I found most of what was happening indefensible. I still do. I too was angry.

While I heard many clerics and even lay people at times explain away the abuse crisis as 'a thing of the past', or 'a few bad apples', there were some key moments that blew it wide open for me. I chose to educate myself and read widely on the subject. There were lots of metanoia moments.

One came when watching the film *Spotlight* in 2015 and seeing the list of dioceses around the world where significant numbers of clergy and religious had been credibly found guilty of abuse.

As the credits rolled, the list of countries and cities spanned several screens. I saw my own diocese and the dioceses my parents grew up in.

I heard stories of family members who had been abused by a prolific paedophile priest, a man who was supported by the Church until just months before his death.

I have concluded that I and perhaps most Catholics are simply human beings trying to make sense of the *chiaroscuro* of life through the lens of the mystery of faith.

I wouldn't blame anyone if they felt that the Church, particularly in its response and actions around the Royal Commission into Institutional Responses to Child Sexual Abuse was just asking a bit much, and that this ignorant monolith no longer has a place in modern society.

One priest I spoke to about this book told me that I would be maligned and attacked. He warned me against it and said I would simply be 'defending the bishops'.

I am not and I hope you will read on.

I don't seek to defend the indefensible. Moreover, I wish to propose another way of looking at this fractured institution and to find ways that I might work collectively with others toward renewal. The Church simply cannot remain as it is.

Some might argue that the activity of the Church is no longer an expression of love that seeks the greater good. In fact, they may feel it is the opposite.

Yet analogies about love can still be applied to a broken Church. Hearts have been broken, but perhaps the tools exist to repair them, to perform open heart surgery.

The reason is that love is not all there is in the world. If the Church is in and of the world then, necessarily, the forces of evil and hate will enter it.

Only perfect love drives out fear, and most of us love imperfectly most of the time.

The first and foremost principle of Catholic Social Teaching is that we are all created in the image and likeness of God and with dignity.

While we are fearfully and wonderfully made, we are created differently too.

We are a garden of varied flowers. We grow and love imperfectly. Our stems break, we lose petals. We are crushed underfoot and grow from seeds in the ground again.

We live and move and have our being in God who was revealed in flesh 2,000 years ago, but who is also beyond all seeing. God is love, and God moves within us, but do we listen? Are we attuned to that love?

And so, for all her flaws and faults, I love this Church. My love is a familial love.

One of the spiritual works of mercy is to admonish the sinner, but what if the sin is collective?

Do I give fraternal correction to the institution when there are so many to blame?

My love for the Church makes the pain of failure deeper and more profound, yet I can identify with brokenness and sinfulness, and the sacraments assist me in processing that. I grasp, albeit often unhealthily and tenuously, a sense of my own frailty.

While forgiveness is paramount, there is much in today's church scandals that I cannot defend because I simply cannot fathom the depth of the fall. There is much that makes me just shake my head and stare in silence and rage.

In recent times, I have observed a significant and growing number of Catholic peers, many of whom had practised for their whole lives, leaving the Church. Many of my survey respondents resonated with these feelings, while many were able to find nuance and live in the creative tension:

> I understand why people leave the Church because I did too. But the basic teachings of our Lord and saviour offer hope and salvation in a difficult world. I have found much healing and support in being an active member of my parish. I ignore aspects of the Church I find ridiculous or irritating.

The Director of the Office for the Participation of Women for the Australian Church, Andrea Dean, spoke to this creative tension in her responses to the survey:

> *I do love the play on words of 'practising' Catholic which suggests that no one gets it right but we try to do our best! I miss the experience of community when I move away from Church. I yearn for nourishment in liturgy. I stay because it is part of who I am and at the moment I am in a situation where I have the space and opportunity to enable good things to happen for women . . .*

> *In recent years I have been on the fringe of Parish, partly because I have been travelling a lot but also because many of my friends are disconnected from Parish. I have been in the fortunate situation of being able to graze on the best that the Church has to offer through participating in retreats, conferences, etc. all over Australia.*

So, for many, it takes reflection, often moments of crisis, often a deep wondering to decide to continue in the tradition.

When we view that tradition as one that encompasses all of life's moments, celebrating the ordinary and extraordinary in birth and death and eating at table, we see that there is vulnerability in every moment. We will have our hearts broken as members of this body.

This little book, as its title suggests, looks at all the beautiful things I see in this Church.

It will look at some ugly things, too.

There are times when the ugly seems to overwhelm.

The light and shade, the black, the white, the grey and all the colours, too.

It's not an academic or a theological text.

It is a cathartic text, a journey. A pilgrimage of discovery and a questioning.

It's a shared journey.

I have gathered the thoughts of many, engaging conversation partners who have a wide range of views: women and men, young people and older people, laity, religious, priests, bishops, mothers, fathers, sisters, brothers, academics and high school students. They are all important.

Why do I even care when she, the Church, and her members have hurt so many near, dear and far from me?

Why, for all her faults, does this 2000-year-old tradition still speak deeply to my heart?

Maybe on this journey, you will see places where the tradition has spoken to your heart too. Maybe it will spark in you some communal memory, some good news to purge the darkness, and you might return or discover this faith with new eyes.

> *I am still practising. Why? Because Jesus says: 'Do this in memory of me', and I don't want to forget.* (Survey respondent)

> *I believe in God. My baptismal promise is to witness to Christ's command 'to go out to all the world and share the Good News'.* (Survey respondent)

So here is a story.

Leaning over a cup of white tea, my head resting against my palm, I sat with my 91-year-old Grandma Peg, surrounded by bits and pieces that speak of her faith.

There are photos on the wall of weddings, and there are family photos and an icon of Mother Teresa. Scattered about are a cross, some rosary beads and a copy of the local Catholic newspaper.

We speak easily. Much of what we talk about is the Church. Not in theological terms, mind you, rather, more about the different people and characters that populate our parishes.

I tell her about my book project and ask her about her own faith. I cite the scandals in the Church, the rules, the challenges, but at the end of the day, I want to know why she stays.

She smiles, no doubt wondering why this grandchild of hers has such obscure interests.

Very few of her numerous grandchildren 'darken the doorstep' of a Catholic church; even her own kids, baby boomers, have opted out.

I was different. My father used to describe my brother and me in our early twenties thus: 'Well, one of them has been hit with a beer bottle and the other one's been hit by a Bible.'

I could never really work out which of us was which to be honest, but it was an interesting observation.

Grandma's response to my questioning was one of the most simple, honest and forthright that you will find in these pages:

> *Well, I don't worry too much about the priests and that. It's because of my faith in God. I like going to mass, I enjoy it. Actually, the only days I don't go to mass are Sundays and Mondays.*

Lots of the survey respondents said similar things:

> *As a way of living in the world, Catholicism is as much a part of me as any of my physical senses. Whatever scandals there are, whatever sins and failings of the community, stopping being Catholic would be like electing to lose an eye. It would impoverish me, and the way I see the world.*

Another wrote:

> *I was raised in a family of practicing Catholics, which I am grateful for. Although I have seen the broken church, I have seen the hope beyond that. It took a while, but I am no longer blind to the beauty of the church, and the potential it has.*
>
> *So many times, I have been close to leaving the church because of the scandals, the lack of young people, or the bad music. For a long time, I stayed a part of the Catholic Church because I thought doing otherwise would disappoint my Catholic parents. However, although I will never excuse the terrible things the Church has done, which continue to disgrace me and break my heart, I have learnt that we must never lose sight of the Eucharist, because it remains the world's single hope.*

Grandma raised ten children between 1946 and the late 1970s. She still has weekly visits from my Aunt Minnie who was born with a disability. In her sixtieth year, Minnie still delights and baffles us all.

'We had the Second Rite of Reconciliation the other night at the church', Grandma says. 'I wanted to go to Fr Kevin, and he was in the little confessional box, so I asked your aunt if she wanted to go in with me.'

My aunt was not at all enamoured of the suggestion.

'No way. I'm not going in there!' said Minnie, wary of the little dark box, and quite content to wait in a pew.

Grandma laughs at the memory.

'She's lucky, she's one of God's little angels who is incapable of sinning, so we better be nice to her 'cos she'll be up there telling St Peter whether to let us into heaven or not', explains Grandma fondly.

Many can articulate why it is that they cling onto faith in a flailing church; for others it is all in the mystery. Some can use big words to describe their theological understanding of one doctrine or another.

Some have few words beyond the rote-learned prayers from the penny catechism.

Others I asked had similar answers to my grandma's, not necessarily dependent on their generation. As mentioned, an online survey on the subject provided some quite remarkable answers.

Many people loved the tradition, but saw that things need to unfold in new ways. Others felt that while there were challenging things about being Catholic today, it was worth it for the truth they found. Some sample responses are included below.

One said:

> *The gift of the Eucharist is paramount. That it has tradition, that this Church stems from the very Apostles themselves and that Jesus began this Church. The aesthetic beauty of the Mass and the classlessness of the church. It isn't for the rich or the poor, nor for gay or straight, nor for any group—but for all. The gift of the sacraments especially confession is beautiful.*

Another said:

> *I'm still Catholic because where else would I go? It's part of my identity. Whenever I go to other churches I feel like an outsider, no matter how much I like them. I'm not fussed about the Church's teaching. I'm more interested in God's. There's often overlap but not always.*

Another spoke of the Church as a home:

> *I stay because I have found a home within the Catholic Church. I know that my home is broken. The fathers of this home are just as broken as I. I stay in the Catholic Church because I can come to the literal presence of Jesus in the Eucharist and bring to him my own personal sufferings.*

For me, the answer isn't simple. I'm about three generations removed from my grandmother, who always seems young to me, even at ninety-one.

Hers was one of the last generations to unquestioningly attend church. Grandma was born in 1927. I was born in 1982. She grew up with 'Faith of Our Fathers' and 'Hail Queen of Heaven', and I grew up with 'I Am the Bread of Life' and 'Shout To the Lord'.

There are of course moments in which the question of the role of Catholicism has edged to the forefront of societal discourse.

On the day in 2012 when then Prime Minister Julia Gillard announced that there would be a Royal Commission into Institutional Responses to Child Sexual Abuse in Australia, I received no less than thirty-eight media enquiries to my mobile phone.

I worked for the Australian Catholic Bishops Conference that year and it was a fraught time.

I was not a spokesperson and the bishops did not perform to a script.

In truth, mostly all I could do was pass on some calls and be something of a glorified press secretary, but it was a time of learning much about the workings of the Church.

I had been no stranger to similar calls since beginning my time in this role in 2009, and throughout the five years that I worked there, there were more calls regarding historical abuse than just about any other subject. It is the issue that continues to provoke strong feelings throughout the Australian Church.

This was a moment where the Church was called to conversion.

It cannot be understated how much learning needed to occur in the attitudes of many of the Church leaders; many of them did learn, and some are still on a steep learning curve.

I certainly learned things in those years, many of which I would like to forget. I learned of sin and scandal, I learned of my own weakness.

I learned to open my eyes and ask more questions.

The scandals have had a huge role to play in the exodus of some people from the church, and yet they have also had a considerable impact on people's deepening of faith in Christ rather than in the institution.

A local priest, one of the younger priests in an archdiocese, spoke of the very deep impact that the clergy abuse scandals have had on tarnishing the reputation of the church.

He has identified the paradox of being willingly bound to the traditional institution while acknowledging its problematic baggage.

> *I am a priest, and therefore, the Church has ordained me, so on a personal level it splits you in two. Because on one hand it's the institution that gave you the beautiful contact with people, but it has also destroyed lives. So, the institution is on the nose, but it's the institution that has ordained me. Obviously, there's a huge amount of shame, disillusionment, anger, humiliation. People are confused. And to be brutally honest, the words paedophile and priest have become interchangeable. It's gut-wrenching.*
>
> *In some ways, the men who should have been feared in decades past were trusted, and now the ones who can be trusted are feared. So, it is a complete reversal.*
>
> *That said, in some ways, we've never been healthier, as in, the emperor has got no clothes, he's been exposed. What's happened now is that we've all had to grow up because you cannot in these circumstances be ambivalent or lukewarm in your faith, or it wouldn't survive. So, we've had to go deeper. I honestly think though that this is a 100-year process, decades and decades of long hard processes.*

It is with comments like this that I personally resonate. The scandals have had the paradoxical effect of strengthening my faith in Christ while questioning the institutional structures. I believe in Christ, and while I see the need for some level of structure and governance, much of it needs dismantling from the top down. The scandals have helped me refine my ideals of the kind of church I would like to be a part of.

All the Beautiful Things is the title I have chosen for this book, because I want to talk about some of the beauty (in the brokenness) that I have found in Christianity, and more specifically, Catholicism.

What is beauty?

I want to talk a bit about why I think it matters, or why it is worthwhile, for us to remain in the beautiful tension that is the Catholic Church, as uncomfortable as it can be.

Much of this will be done through story, because it's the stories of beauty and pain that make up a life and give us hope. 'Beauty scatters the seed of hope in us,'[6] says Benedictine Sr Joan Chittister.

And so, with stories I will start, and I will liberally sprinkle them throughout, like salt or spice in a melting pot, or like hundreds and thousands sprinkled to make that great children's party staple, fairy bread.

---

6. Attributed to Sr. Joan Chittister OSB, Pennsylvania, USA.

Yet, the Catholic Church's history, including its recent history, is no fairy tale. Some may say of late that it's a nightmare.

At the very least, at times, it can resemble Hogwarts, a medieval court complete with jesters and robes, and odd and archaic machinations.

Fr Andrew Greeley in his book *The Catholic Imagination* describes Catholicism this way:

> Catholics live in an enchanted world, a world of statues and holy water, stained glass and votive candles, saints and religious medals, rosary beads and holy pictures. But these Catholic paraphernalia are mere hints of a deeper and more pervasive religious sensibility which inclines Catholics to see the holy lurking in creation. As Catholics, we find our houses and our world haunted by a sense that the objects, events and persons of daily life are revelations of grace.[7]

Some of us in the Catholic Church probably do live in something of a fairyland. To me, it's always been important to balance reason and the intellect with the mystery and often folkloric traditions.

We need to see the holy if we are to find beauty, and this can be hard amid the ugly scars of the evil perpetrated against thousands of young people by paedophilia and abuse.

We must acknowledge it, and I don't think the institution, or our leaders, have gone far enough by any stretch.

We shouldn't move on from this space yet, not until every tear has been wiped away.

We need to don sackcloth and ashes.

And how do we wipe away these tears, heal these wounds?

A story, or more likely a legend, is told about St Teresa of Avila, the second female Doctor of the Church and great Spanish mystic.

During her life, particularly while living in her Carmelite convent, St Teresa had many mystical visions.

Legend has it that one day the devil appeared to her, but he was disguised as Jesus Christ. Teresa knew instantly that he was the devil in disguise and was asked by him how she knew. 'I knew because you had no wounds.'

---

7. Andrew Greeley, *The Catholic Imagination* (Berkeley, Calif: University of California Press, 2001), 1.

So indeed, a Church without wounds does not reflect the person of Christ.

That said, such symbolism can sound apologetic. Perhaps it sounds as though I am defending the Church and placing the albatross back around the necks of those who have been hurt by the Church. Perhaps this story reads as though we must continue to suffer for this Church and never obtain any joy or healing in this life. But that would be too simplistic a perspective.

One lay commentator, George Weigel, wrote in the introduction to his book *The Courage to be Catholic*:

> Like every community, the Catholic Church is a Church of sinners. Its spiritual rhythms repeat the ancient biblical cycle of failure, repentance, penance, forgiveness and reconciliation. Yet even in a Church that knows a lot about sin, some acts of wickedness still retain their capacity to shock. The sexual abuse of minors by priests—men traditionally called 'Father'—is one such kind of wickedness. So is the failure of bishops—shepherds, in the ancient image—to guard the flock against predators, especially predators from within the household of faith.[8]

I was recently sitting with my dad who is a long-time member of one of Australia's best representations of faith in action, the Society of St Vincent de Paul.

Dad spent his twenties and thirties volunteering in men's shelters, often having to lift men into a shower when they arrived drunk and soiled at the shelter door.

He would hand them a coffee and pass them a blanket to warm up although the rule said that those who showed up intoxicated could not have a bed until they were sober.

He would have to wash them at times and, knowing my dad, it was probably a bit rough, but nonetheless, done with a heart for justice.

We were discussing Vincentian spirituality in the context of a local parish conference which had passed some harsh criticism of another person in their recent meeting.

---

8. George Weigel, *The Courage To Be Catholic: Crisis, Reform and the Future of the Church* (New York: Basic Books, 2007), i.

Both dad and I have a reasonably well-developed sense of social justice. We were angry about the judgement and were debriefing about its effects. I nearly fell off my chair when my father proclaimed: 'They are ALL part of the rich tapestry of life.'

If you were to meet my dad, you would understand how unusual such a statement is, and I can only say that it was either the Holy Spirit or a few too many sherbets at the pub that led to it. But it got me thinking.

The rich tapestry, the stained-glass window, the seamless garment. These are all images I will refer to in this book. The tapestry has many coloured threads. Some of the threads are coarse in nature, thickly embroidered onto the backing. Some are smooth, shining with different hues. Some threads get slowly whittled away by the family cat as she sharpens her claws. And so are human beings.

And then there is the image which many associate with majestic churches, the stained-glass window. And, wouldn't you know it: A stained-glass window is literally made up of pieces of broken glass.

Colleagues and I have often cringed when bishops or priests are interviewed by the media and we have watched as the journalist has inevitably placed these men in front of a stained-glass window—perhaps to enhance the image of holiness or, more likely, to solidify a cliché.

The stained glass, however, is quite beautiful on its own—made up of many different colours and shapes—just like the people of God.

In March 2013, the eyes of the world were on a chimney top in Rome. A fat seagull was perched across this important chimney, and at times seemed to be peering down into it.

What transpired that night was, to put it mildly, unexpected.

A little-known Argentinian Jesuit, Jorge Mario Bergoglio, emerged onto the balcony of St Peter's Basilica with a small wave and simple vestments.

Bergoglio wore the same pectoral cross that he had worn in the slums of Buenos Aires and the halls of power. He had chosen the name Francis, after his brother Cardinal Cláudio Hummes had urged Bergoglio to 'not forget about the poor' once he was elected Pope.

Pope Francis' first Apostolic Exhortation *The Joy of the Gospel—Evangelii Gaudium* outlined, in many ways, the blueprint for his papacy.

Like John XXIII, Francis seems to know he won't have a marathon papacy like John Paul II. He may not even get Benedict's eight years.

So, he switched into gear quickly and has charmed many and irritated not a few.

He wrote:

> I prefer a Church which is bruised, hurting and dirty because it has been out on the streets, rather than a Church which is unhealthy from being confined and from clinging to its own security ... *More than by fear of going astray, my hope is that we will be moved by the fear of remaining shut up within structures which give us a false sense of security, within rules which make us harsh judges, within habits which make us feel safe, while at our door people are starving and Jesus does not tire of saying to us:* 'Give them something to eat.' (Mk 6:37).[9]

Francis uses a lot of symbolism and imagery throughout his Apostolic Exhortation. This is his game plan and, in simple terms, I want to be around to see it.

The ancient words and traditions of Catholicism have a rich beauty to them. But in new and uncertain times, when much of that culture has led to a cover up of evil, how do we repair this house?

It cannot be done just through words. Reconciliation, redemption and renewal cannot happen simply by paying lip-service. While there is some doubt as to its origin, St Francis of Assisi is quoted along these lines: 'Be always preaching the Gospel, and if necessary, use words.'

We need to go beyond words, and pastoral letters, and written apologies.

Action is required, and hopefully in the pages of this book, you will find some inspiration and support to take that action.

In 2020, the Catholic Church in this country will convene a Plenary Council, a forum that will hopefully unite Catholics and be designed so that people in every diocese might work collegially toward renewal and rebuilding.

---

9. Pope Francis, *Evangelii Gaudium: Apostolic Exhortation on the Proclamation of the Gospel in Today's World (24 November 2013)* at <http://w2.vatican.va/content/francesco/en/apost_exhortations/documents/papa-francesco_esortazione-ap_20131124_evangelii-gaudium.html>. Accessed 9 September 2019.

Will it be the be all and end all to the questions people have? It's highly unlikely. It will likely only be a starting point, or a mid-point on a journey.

I suspect it will not settle all the internal debates or quell the voices of those who seek change.

I suspect that only those who still have a shred of hope will pick it up. It's possible people will think I'm deluded to share the ideas and thoughts presented in this book. Yet, here it is. A humble offering. One that might be unpopular, but that I think needs to be put out there, for what it's worth.

As a profoundly universal tradition (indeed the meaning of the word 'Catholic' is 'universal') each member of the body of Christ will experience Catholicism differently.

While the rituals and the sacraments and the celebration of the mass have a sense of conformity wherever you go, the cultural aspects of a life lived in faith vary widely.

Therefore, my own Catholicism, my Christianity, is in some fundamental ways different even to those closest family members who were first in initiating me into this belief system.

On a day to day basis, Catholicism is important to me, and so are the little rituals. The breadth of spiritual traditions and devotions can mean there is something that suits all personality types.

Some find deep comfort, for example, in praying the Rosary or saying the Divine Office; others may be more inclined toward imaginative contemplation, or praise and worship.

While it's important not to be 'cafeteria Catholics' or 'buffet Catholics'—picking and choosing the teachings and dogmas that suit us and our lifestyles—there are different expressions of spirituality which are all valid and there are a variety of ways in which faith can be expressed.

In my own journey, it is precisely this breadth that means no other system makes sense to me.

Audrey Assad, a Catholic songwriter wrote something similar on Twitter in 2017, and it is with this I will end Chapter One.

> It's really starting to hit home to me that many Christians see the church more as a country club than a hospital. It started to hit home to me when Mike Brown was shot and now my people are viewed (Syrians/Arabs) as barely human by people whose God became [a] Middle Eastern human and died

crucified. I've tried not to stay here, I've tried to leave. I've tried not to be a Christian anymore, but I love the church, it turns out. It's the thorn in my side, the pillow under my head, and my mother and my drunk uncle. Some tell me all day long that I don't belong [to] her with my suspect politics or my disappointing lack of Thomism. But I am staying with you.[10]

I concur. Let me, and my friends, tell you why.

---

10. @audreyassad, 'It's really starting to hit home to me that many Christians see the church more as a country club than a hospital . . .' Accessed 31 January, 2017.

Chapter Two
Of Saints and Sinners

Don't call me a saint, I don't want to be dismissed that easily.[1]

In sixth grade, like many children at Catholic schools, I was asked to choose a saint for my Confirmation.

It wasn't a particularly well-considered moment, in fact it's an irony never lost on me that my mother, a catechist who prepared government school students for the Sacrament of Confirmation, had such trust in the Catholic school system that she thought I'd be well prepared for this sacrament.

It would be a lie to say that I pored over books on the lives of the saints, carefully considering my choice and praying for inspiration.

For me, it ended up as a bit of a competition.

For several years, I had in mind the patron saint of music, St Cecilia, as my planned namesake. But when I mentioned that to my best friend at the time, she jumped on it, and wouldn't budge.

I settled for St Thérèse of Lisieux, with little appreciation for the depth of this Doctor of the Church and, indeed, less understanding of what she signalled for me at that very time.

If I had my time again, I'd have a long list of people from whom I might choose, and far more idea of why.

Saints, whether canonised or not, give us models and behaviours to emulate. They also, and more importantly, point to Christ as their strength.

---

1. Dorothy Day quoted in B J Gonzalvo, *Lessons in Leadership from the Saints: Called to Holiness, Called to Lead* (Bloomington, IN: WestBow Press, 2017), 4.

Indeed, the Catholic Church's reverence for and focus on the Communion of Saints can often be what leads to ridicule by people from other Christian denominations.

Many wrongly believe that we worship and reverence saints instead of going straight to the source.

And yet, when properly understood, the saints are one of the very beautiful things about this Catholic tradition.

Twentieth-century servant of God Dorothy Day is famously quoted as saying: 'Don't call me a saint, I don't want to be dismissed that easily.'[2]

She didn't want people to use her heroic virtue as an excuse not to do something, or not to listen to where she was coming from.

She didn't want to give people an excuse not to do anything with their unique vocational calls.

Day felt that being referred to as a saint gave people the sense that they could dismiss her as holy, and that they, in their day-to-day lives, were unable to live out the same virtues that she saw as so fundamental to her call, and to the call of all Christians.

When you really start learning about the Communion of Saints, you will notice (particularly if you dig deeply beyond the hagiographical tales) that there are hopeful stories of people who, like us, struggled against sin.

The saints (and we can include those who haven't yet been formally recognised by the Church in our study) while modelling certain characteristics that we might emulate, all have their back stories, their moments of conversion, their often-scandalous pasts.

There is a helpful phrase that I often go back to: 'There is no saint without a past and no sinner without a future.'

Indeed, one of my favourite conversion stories is that of St Ignatius of Loyola, the founder of the Jesuits.

In 2011, I found myself in the chapel in Loyola, Spain where St Ignatius received many of his initial visions, a place where he was convalescing after a battle wound.

St Ignatius' memoir, *A Pilgrim's Testament*, starts along the following lines: 'Up to his twenty-sixth year he was a man given to worldly vanities.'[3]

---

2. Dorothy Day quoted in B J Gonzalvo, *Lessons in Leadership from the Saints: Called to Holiness, Called to Lead* (Bloomington, IN: WestBow Press, 2017), 4.
3. Saint Ignatius of Loyola and Joseph Tylenda, *A Pilgrim's Journey: The Autobiography of Ignatius of Loyola* (Revised edition) (San Francisco: Ignatius Press, 2001), 37.

Some of us need a bigger nudge than others to change our path in life; for Ignatius, it came in the form of a cannon ball to the leg.

As he convalesced in Loyola in the Basque country, he found himself without entertainment, and requested some books to read.

Desiring fantasy tales of knights and princesses, instead he was given *The Life of Christ* by Ludolph of Saxony and *Flowers of the Saints*.

Over time, as he re-read and made notes on these texts, he started to imagine himself as a warrior for Christ, instead of a warrior on the battlefield.

He went on to become the founder the Catholic Church's largest religious order, the Society of Jesus.

Our church, indeed, the entire Christian story is centred around the concept of redemption.

Many of the saints, canonised or not, had pasts worthy of soap operas and reality TV.

You might perhaps think of St Augustine of Hippo, who famously said: 'Lord, grant me chastity, but not yet.'

Then there is Thomas Merton who fathered a child while still at university, before he went on to spend most of the rest of his life in a Trappist monastery in Kentucky.

Others, like St Ignatius, had a criminal record after being arrested for brawling in the street.

The Irish ascetic, Matthew Talbot, after whom Sydney's hostel for the homeless is named, struggled his entire life with alcoholism.

Dorothy Day had several affairs in her youth, went through the pain of abortion, and never married the father of her daughter, Tamar.

These are just a few of the saints that give me hope.

And of course, sainthood is not always well understood. As mentioned, one of the criticisms levelled at Catholics is that we pray to saints instead of straight to God.

This is not actually correct because, in fact, we ask for the saints to intercede on our behalf with Jesus and the Father. This in no way diminishes Jesus' importance.

Indeed, the Communion of Saints is made up of people who had deep and fruitful relationships with Jesus through prayer; people who point us to Christ.

Between the first World Youth Day in the 1980s and 2002, this event, attended by millions of young people, would always have that moment of papal worship where people would shout out in an almost chant-like chorus 'John Paul II, we love you'.

John Paul II, the founder of World Youth Day, had such a cult following among young people that they would often forget the reason they were attending these gatherings—focusing on the Holy Father.

John Paul II would always respond to this multilingual mantra by proclaiming: 'No, no! Jesus', pointing his finger in the air. He was at pains to demonstrate that these events were not about him as the Pope, but about Jesus.

He saw it as his mission to point us to Christ.

Sometimes the cultural focus on Mary in many countries, particularly Latin America and parts of Asia, can also confuse people, and it is something we should learn about and try to communicate better as a Church.

For me, personally, there are some non-canonised saints whose stories resonate deeply.

Mev Puleo is one such example.

In 2008, I ordered a book over the internet called *The Book of Mev*.[4]

I came across it after having read Robert Ellsberg's fantastic treasury of women saints, *Blessed among All Women: Women Saints, Prophets, and Witnesses for Our Time*.[5]

In the pages of Ellsberg's book, I read about each of the women he profiled—from the feisty Teresa of Avila who reformed the Carmelite order to Catherine of Siena who famously said: 'Be who God meant you to be, and you will set the world afire.'

However, it was a lesser-known American woman whose story stood out. Perhaps it was because her own journey and gifts seemed to resonate so much with my own. She was American journalist, theologian and photojournalist Mev Puleo.

Puleo was an advocate for justice whose conversion to the cause of the poor came about on a family trip to Brazil.

On an air-conditioned tour bus, Puleo and her family were driving up Mount Corcovado, which overlooks Rio de Janeiro, approaching the famous statue of Christ the King.

Looking out one window, she could see luxurious condos, swimming pools and other lifestyle excesses. On the other side were Rio's notorious favelas where people survive on less than $2 a day.

---

4. Mark Chmiel, *The Book of Mev* (New York: Xlibris, 2006).
5. Robert Ellsberg, *Blessed among All Women: Women, Saints, Prophets, and Witnesses for Our Time* (London: Darton Longman & Todd, 2006).

Puleo was so moved by this paradox and contradiction, she vowed to use her talents from then on in service of the poor.

She travelled throughout Latin America interviewing activists and liberation theologians, and her book, *The Struggle Is One: Voices and Visions of Liberation*,[6] is a testimony from those she interviewed, in Portuguese and Spanish, about how they were seeking to live out the Gospel message of freedom.

Just two years after its publication, Mev lost a battle with terminal brain cancer at the age of thirty-two, leaving behind her husband of just three years, Mark Chmiel, and an extraordinary legacy.

Mev was entirely herself, and entirely committed to the values she had come to believe in. She actively sought to discover how she might use her own unique gifts and talents to give glory to God.

Fr James Martin speaks of this sense of realisation in his book *Becoming Who You Are*.[7] He uses the unusual lives of certain religious figures such as Thomas Merton to explain that being exactly who you were made to be would, in the end, be most likely to produce 'saintly' results.

The business of making saints is an interesting, long and expensive process, so most people we view as 'saintly' will never be canonised in the official sense.

There are people I have known personally whose names will never be read, along with a list of their greatest deeds, at the Vatican.

I think of my music teacher, Meg, who taught me for eleven years and never lost her temper once. This on its own is a saintly feat.

She had long given up the practice of any religion, but day after day she showed a dedicated patience for her temperamentally varied piano students.

In Rome, in 2010, I attended the canonisation ceremony of Mary MacKillop and five other saints. Canonised as St Mary of the Cross, MacKillop was Australia's first saint and she truly embodied the Aussie battler spirit.

Born on that most iconic of Melbourne streets, Brunswick Street in the suburb of Fitzroy, she knew poverty, and she knew that she wanted to respond to that. Later, she would be quoted as saying: 'Never see a need without doing something about it.'

---

6. Mev Puleo, *The Struggle Is One: Voices and Visions of Liberation* (Albany, NY: State University of New York Press, 1994).
7. James Martin, *Becoming Who You Are: Insights on the True Self from Thomas Merton and Other Saints* (Mahwah, NJ: HiddenSpring, 2006).

MacKillop felt a call early on and established (despite significant opposition) the Sisters of St Joseph of the Sacred Heart, an order that still boasts a numerous membership today.

With her unstinting heart for the poor, and clothed in a brown and white habit, she set up schools across the most impoverished rural areas of Australia.

Her foundation now works in Peru, Timor, New Zealand and Brazil among other places.

The canonisation process was an interesting thing for me to witness. I had a bird's eye view in the press gallery, a scaffolded structure where journalists with telephoto lenses could mount their gear and file their stories.

I watched as journalists flocked to the well-known cardinals and bishops they sighted in Vatican square, often not noticing the plainly-clothed sisters with bright teal scarves—the Josephite sisters of today.

I remember a moment of grace or perception during the ceremony that has stayed with me since.

I had sighted an older couple from my own parish in Australia and said hello to them before climbing up the stairs to watch the canonisation ceremony, a liturgy that would last almost four hours.

My stomach gave a dive, and panic set in.

It was as though I realised I was in the presence of holiness, and I felt (as John the Baptist put it) unworthy to tie the sandals of many of the crowd of pilgrims who had gathered for the occasion.

Sobered by the experience, I was quiet and contemplative for most of the mass. I simply didn't feel like I had the right to be there.

Mary Mackillop had struggled with Church authorities, even to the point where she was excommunicated at one point by a crazed bishop who then begged her forgiveness on his deathbed.

It was recollections like these that slowly consoled me and made me realise that my responses to these feelings of shame and guilt and unworthiness were as important as the feelings themselves.

Days later, still suffering kind of a shame hangover, I had started to think deeply about what God was really calling me to in life.

As part of an already-planned add-on to my itinerary, I had work to do for the upcoming World Youth Day in Spain. Together with a small group of church lay leaders, I would be touring regions of that beautiful country in what was called 'the familiarisation'.

As part of that tour, we would see Toledo, Segovia, Avila, and parts of the outskirts of Madrid. I found myself particularly moved in Avila, where St Teresa had founded the Discalced Carmelites, and from where John of the Cross had written. Spain is a good place for saints. It's influence in the Church over the centuries has seen it become the breeding ground for a vast range of religious expressions, from the Dominicans to the Jesuits, and from the Discalced Carmelites to, more recently, Verbum Dei, the Neocatechumenal Way and Opus Dei.

It was while travelling in Spain that year that I discovered that St Ignatius and St Teresa had been canonised on the same day back in the 1600s, even though both were people of controversy during their lives.

It was here that the scales fell from my eyes, allowing me to see things as they really were. The beauty of the communion of saints is not in pious relics, but in the battles and struggles they faced, even with their beloved Church.

One of my survey respondents seems to agree with me on this point, because when asked about what the Church meant to them, they wrote:

> *The Church reminds me that as a member of a community of saints and sinners, I am not perfect and that I need a community to keep me accountable. Finally, the Church enables me to love and hope beyond the horizons of this world.*

And so, to me it seems likely that the saints present in our own lives will likely be the ones who rebuild this fragile institution.

Recently, I have been listening to a new podcast called *Jesuitical*,[8] produced by America Media, a Jesuit Media ministry in New York City. At the end of each episode, the three young hosts ask their guests who they would canonise if they had the chance. The guests can choose anyone they like, living or dead, Catholic or non-Catholic.

About a year ago, they interviewed the Christian writer Rachel Held Evans, a woman from an evangelical background, and author of four extraordinary books on her search for the true meaning of Church.

---

8. America Media, *Jesuitical* at <https://www.americamagazine.org/jesuitical>. Accessed 9 September 2019.

As I was finishing writing this book, the thirty-seven-year-old passed away suddenly, and I found myself returning to her interview with America Media's podcast Jesuitical, and to some of her words.

There are few writers who have resonated with me so deeply when it comes to making sense of a faith of contradictions, and this quote of hers really stood out to me: 'The church is God saying: "I'm throwing a banquet, and all these mismatched, messed-up people are invited. Here, have some wine."'[9]

Rachel Held Evans, pray for us.

So indeed, as I complete this reflection on the gift of the saints to the Church, I would argue that it is their example that will ultimately convince us of both our own worthiness and of the worthiness of holding on to this often fragile, messy relic.

It will be through works of mercy, prayer, outreach and compassion that we will slowly replace the crumbling mortar with living answers.

It will be those people of justice, many of whom will never be formally recognised, who I hope will turn this barque of Peter around.

---

9. Rachel Held Evans, *Searching for Sunday: Loving, Leaving, and Finding the Church* (Nashville: Thomas Nelson, 2015), 153.

Chapter Three
The Gift of the Sacraments

The sacraments are tangible ways to represent intangible ideas: The idea of a Saviour, of a sacrifice, of body and blood so many centuries ago, fills our senses and invades our present when our fingers break bread and our mouths fill with wine. We don't experience this connection, this remembering, this intimate memory and celebration of Christ, only at the altar. We experience it, or at least we could, every time the bread and wine are present—essentially, every time we are fed . . . My friend Shane says the genius of Communion, of bread and wine, is that bread is the food of the poor and wine the drink of the privileged, and that every time we see those two together, we are reminded of what we share instead of what divides us.[1]

Sitting in front of the Blessed Sacrament, a group of young adults have gathered for adoration. They sing the song 'Jesus, My Lord, My God, My All'.

It is this act of faith that they make each week, praying a rosary, occasionally joining together in praise and worship, and sharing a meal that builds communion and community.

They always use this hymn because it best expresses for them the mystery of why they stay, and the challenge in doing so. Its words are old, but its truth remains.

While all Christian traditions have a sacramental life, the Catholic Church takes it up a notch with a sense of ritual and tradition that dates to our Jewish roots. There is a beautiful sense of continuity and

---

1. Shauna Niequist, *Bread & Wine: A Love Letter to Life around the Table, with Recipes* (Grand Rapids, Mich: Zondervan, 2013).

memory, and a very integrated way of celebrating these moments that gives them a unique importance.

The word 'sacrament' originally came from the Ecclesiastical Latin '*sacramentum*', from the derivative '*sacer*' meaning 'sacred' or 'holy'.

There are seven possible sacraments we can receive throughout our lives of faith, but few of us in the Catholic tradition will receive all seven.

Two, for example, necessarily cancel out each other: Marriage and Holy Orders. By choosing one of these vocations, we cancel out the other, at least that is the case at the current moment.

Our sacramental journey usually starts with Baptism and, if we are born into this faith, it usually happens some time in our first year of life. Baptism is followed by Reconciliation, First Communion (Eucharist) and Confirmation. Then, the order is a bit more flexible. The remaining sacraments are Holy Orders—if you choose to be a priest—Marriage, and Anointing of the Sick.

Some priests will joke about the sacramental life of Catholics of this generation. They jest that there are those who come to Church for the simple rituals of hatch, match and dispatch, that is: baptism, weddings and funerals, but rarely darken the doorstep of a church at any other time.

Fr Richard Leonard SJ recently published a book with this title: *Hatch, Match and Dispatch*.[2] It is a book on the sacraments; a cogent argument in favour of these rituals and their power.

It is in the sacraments that much beauty can be found, and a pleasing sense of ritual than honours life's steps, life's important moments.

At Baptism we are initiated into the family of God, in the name of the Father and the Son and the Holy Spirit. Water is poured on our heads, and we are blessed with holy oils.

This is followed, at least in the Australian Church by the Sacrament of Reconciliation, generally made at the age of eight or nine, although goodness knows there aren't many of us committing mortal sins at those tender ages.

We make our First Communion usually in third grade, a year after confessing our sins. Once again, it's unlikely that we grasp the holiness of the moment when we are given the body and blood of Christ

---

2. Richard Leonard, *Hatch, Match and Dispatch: A Catholic Guide to Sacraments* (New York: Paulist Press, 2019).

for the first time. In truth, I avoided the wine (the blood of Christ) for many years because the strong taste was not to my liking. A side note here, I no longer struggle with this aversion.

Confirmation is sadly often referred to as an 'exit sacrament', and few who make their Confirmation in Australian parishes continue their practice after this stage.

It's perhaps something we could learn from the protestant traditions, where Confirmation and Baptism both happen at once, at an age of relatively more reason.

Then, of course, there are the sacraments that we may or may not take part in.

One survey respondent spoke of the paradox of finding both unity and pain in sacramentality:

> *Sacraments are a focal point, they bring together the community of practice. However, some sacraments can also be a point of constant pain, remembering so many who are invited around the table, [but who] are given the messages to receive whatever crumbs . . . fall off it, or are made to feel that they are not worth the dignity and or have not [the] right to partake around the table.*

Another spoke of how difficult it was to appreciate the Eucharist because of poorly celebrated liturgy:

> *Eucharist is too often meaningless due to poor celebration and a community that does not embrace and welcome.*

Indeed, few of us make all the sacraments available to us, and once we have made the sacraments for the first time, some of them do not continue to sustain us for various reasons. Sometimes we deny ourselves the sacraments, and sometimes they are denied to us.

Then there are those which cancel one another out. If I make the Sacrament of Marriage, it is unlikely that I will then be allowed to make the sacrament of Holy Orders—that is, become a nun or a priest.

Few of us perhaps think of Baptism as a sacrament of redemption. After all, in the Catholic tradition, Baptism usually happens in the first few years of life. What possible sins can a child of just one month have committed from which they need to be cleansed. In fact, however, Baptism is all about initiation and redemption.

About a decade ago, I attended an ordination to the priesthood. If you are ever looking for a moving moment of liturgy, attending an ordination to the priesthood is one way to get that feeling.

Most ordinations have a poignancy about them—the ordinand is literally and figuratively laying down his life to serve the people of God in the Church.

Often, it's that moment where the Litany of the Saints is sung, and the man lies prostrate on the floor in front of the bishop that is most touching.

During this particular ordination, the young man stood up to give a speech at the end of the service. He thanked his parents, as you do, and said something that has never left me:

> *I first want to thank you for the gift of life, and secondly, for the greatest gift you have given me in my life, which was my Baptism into the Catholic Church.*

How very profound. The initiation and welcome, even before we are conscious of it, into the people of God.

I agree with him that my Baptism and subsequent Catholic upbringing have been two of the foundational and most important gifts I have been given.

In the process of writing this book, I attended a baptism of a dear friend's baby. She and her fiancé had been waiting for almost two years for an annulment of his first marriage.

The beautiful way in which they were blessed and welcomed by the church community was palpable. No one asked them questions, no one cared if they were married or not. They were married happily in the church a year later, surrounded by family and friends.

Pope Francis, too, has modelled this same extension of mercy as he has administered the sacraments.

A story is told of him taking pity on Anna Romano, thirty-five, who wrote to him in the Vatican explaining she had discovered the man she was pregnant by was married.

In his unique style, Pope Francis chose to reach out to her by personal phone call. When interviewed by Italy's paper *Corriere della sera*, Anna told the story, saying 'at the beginning I thought it was a joke, but then he referred to the letter, which only my best friend and my parents knew about'.

Romano wanted to keep her child, but was under enormous pressure from outside.

She told the Pope that she was afraid that no priest would baptise her illegitimate child.

In his candid way, the Pope promised he would baptise her baby if she couldn't find a priest and affirmed her in her decision in favour of life.[3]

There are many such stories about Pope Francis, and it reinforces the idea that sacraments generally are moments for grace, redemption and homecoming.

The touch of a priest's hand on the head of a penitent who has confessed their worst sins; the moment of receiving Christ's body in the Eucharist; the drops of oil and water on the head of a baby; an anointing touch of oil on a frail, elderly hand; the joining of two people together in matrimony; or the laying down in front of the altar during an ordination ceremony. These are just a few of the moments of sacrament.

But there is sacramental living more generally.

Breaking bread together, performing works of mercy, blessing others with our time, building community.

Ultimately, the best Catholics, those who truly live out their faith in word and deed will be those who not only attend the Eucharist but wash the feet of the poor; they will be those who not only confess their sins to a priest but give bread to the hungry.

They will be those who sing in the choir and scrub the floor; those who adore the Eucharist and visit the sick. The sacraments don't necessarily make us heroic or ask heroism of us. They are available to us in the ordinary and the everyday, and they are indeed the balm of mercy given to us only in the Church.

> Out of the darkness of my life, so much frustrated, I put before you the one great thing to love on earth: the Blessed Sacrament . . . There you will find romance, glory, honour, fidelity, and the true way of all your loves upon earth.[4]

---

3. Vatican Radio, 'Pope Comforts Pregnant Single Woman' at <http://www.archivioradiovaticana.va/storico/2013/09/13/pope_comforts_pregnant_single_woman/in2-728305>. Accessed 9 September 2019.
4. John Ronald Reuel Tolkien, *The Letters of JRR Tolkien* (Boston: Mariner Books, 2000)

It's perhaps the greatest mystery of faith, the idea that Jesus makes himself present to us in the Eucharist, at each celebration of the mass. Few of us can really understand it.

> *I love the Eucharist, being in, with, part of the body of the Christ. It is both transcendent and immanent. Reconciliation restores our souls and our psychological needs.* (Survey respondent)

> *They [the sacraments] help me to remember that I am part of the Body of Christ in a very real way. It's not just my mind—it's my whole person. Bread, wine, fire, water, the laying on of hands, oil, blessing, forgiveness. Real and tangible.* (Survey respondent)

One of my survey respondents was very articulate in his response to whether the sacraments sustained his participation in the Church:

> *The sacramental fullness of Catholicism has been poorly communicated to at least two generations of Catholics and the sublime and luminous nature of Catholic sacramental and liturgical life has in many areas been lost. For me the sacrament of the Eucharist and its place within the wider liturgical life of the Church has over time become increasingly important as an outward sign of the inner reality of being part of the Church.*

And it's true. Such is the mystery and the confusion around this, that even intra-denominational debates continue.

And yet, it is the most magnificent symbol for this book, because Eucharist is the most important part of the mass.

The Eucharist, often referred to as the source and summit of our faith, is beauty in brokenness. Christ's body, broken and shared with all of us, is the most extraordinary gift, and the most difficult paradox we have. This simple and profound moment in the Church's liturgy takes up more than half the celebration of the mass and is celebrated in much the same way whether you are in Cambodia, Chile or Cameroon.

The words—while spoken in different languages—celebrate the same mystery.

And it is done in all ordinariness, in a meal. Christ comes to us in the form of bread and wine, in those most basic of foodstuffs. As Tish Harrison Warren writes in her book *Liturgy of the Ordinary*, for all the pomp and ceremony that can sometimes accompany the rituals of the Church, there is the ordinariness of it all, particularly in the week to week slog of living out our practice of faith.

> Of all the things he could've chosen to be done 'in remembrance' of him, Jesus chose a meal. He could have asked his followers to do something impressive or mystical—climb a mountain, fast for forty days, or have a trippy sweat lodge ceremony— but instead he picks the most ordinary of acts, eating, through which to be present to his people. He says that the bread is his body and the wine is his blood. He chooses the unremarkable and plain, average and abundant, bread and wine.[5]

In the survey I compiled among my friends and acquaintances who practice Catholicism, to find out which areas were of most beauty to them, sacraments were one of the great sustainers of faith.

From a choice of options asking what was the most important element of the Catholic liturgy, almost fifty per cent of those surveyed answered the Eucharist.

For them, that physical reminder each week of the sacrifice of Christ on the cross for us sometimes filled them with a palpable sense of awe. Often too though, there is a sense of nothingness. It's important to be honest here and say that we are not always aware of the reality of what we are experiencing.

The mystery is too great for us to fully grasp or realise. And then of course, sometimes the very thing that helps us get a glimpse of the risen Christ in the Eucharist is the experience of community.

We all are searching for community. Even the most introverted among us need people. We are made to be in communion with others. But we need to find a place to live and exist. Remembrance not only speaks of the importance of remembrance, but indeed, of finding a community of faith, and coming to the table.

The word '*community*' comes from the Latin '*communis*', meaning 'common', 'public', or 'shared by all or many'.

The health of a community has much to do with how much we put into it, and the Church community is called to go above and beyond what is normal in this respect.

---

5. Tish Harrison Warren, *Liturgy of the Ordinary: Sacred Practices in Everyday Life* (Downers Grove, Ill: IVP Books, 2016), 63.

If you have every gone to mass and felt out of communion or felt that there is a rupture in one of your relationships, you will perhaps notice how clear this becomes around the time of the consecration.

I remember a time in a youth group where I would dread the sign of peace because, as young people, we were all fighting and bitching about one another.

There were people that I could not, in good conscience, shake hands with. In truth, I should not have been fronting up to communion each week with such thoughts in my heart, and I deeply regret my actions at this time.

But it taught me a lesson.

When we break bonds, or share a bond, we are changed. This is what being in communion and community is all about.

Do I ever wonder if the Church is all it professes to be, whether it is, in reality, the mystical body of Christ? Absolutely.

Particularly now, it's a time of contradiction. There are so many groups and movements for and against the Church.

There are divisions within the church; there is a variety of styles of worship and spiritualities and forms of prayer. Sometimes those differences do not unite us.

As I surveyed friends and colleagues for this book, and made comments about my own ideas of Church, I was challenged more than once.

Some didn't agree that the Church has any right to speak on public policy or justice anymore. Others think the Church has no credibility left.

When I made a slightly critical comment in my blog about the leadership of the Church in Australia, a bishop was deeply hurt, and sent me a message about how he was tired of being labelled as one of the 'bad apples'.

My sentiment however was shared by many, if not all the survey respondents, although most also saw the Royal Commission and the reportage and uncovering of scandals as an opportunity for redemption.

A woman who holds a senior position at the Bishops Conference Secretariat said the following:

> I can't believe that the Church is going on as if nothing has happened. I feel like it's 'deck chairs on the Titanic'. I'm disappointed, I'm grieving but I am also hopeful that a big shake up will occur.

A sample of other anonymous survey responses follow:

> *I think it's shocking. And it's not at all clear to me that the hierarchy is willing to consider the cultural changes necessary at this point. The crass grip on power has never been clearer.*

> *The Church has a weak human face. We are all sinners. The Church does 500 times more good than evil, unfortunately it is the evil that hits the press.*

> *I feel great sorrow for victims and frustration/despair that so many in the church still fail to understand the dynamics of abuse, and still put concern for power ahead of victims.*

> *Jesus wept for Jerusalem; I think he would be weeping for scandals in the church—he cleared the Temple of the money lenders; he said 'let the children come to me for to such as these belong the Kingdom of heaven' and 'whatever you do to the least of my people you do to Me'. I think the scandals have rocked the faith of many, myself included; but I hope I can see the real church still alive—despite the scandals, especially the child abuse (both sexual and other) which really disgusts me.*

> *If all these scandals teach the Church humility, then the Holy Spirit will have been at work.*

> *I am not surprised, but I am disgusted. I only pray and hope the character of cover-ups is a 'generational' thing, and something that we no longer continue. On the positive side, these revelations are like tilling the soil, to aerate and rebuild for a better yield.*

So, what does this mean for the sacraments? Are the sacraments changed by scandal?

As members of the body of Christ, joined together in communion, it is impossible not to be affected by the Church's recent history. Indeed, the Sacrament of Reconciliation has, even in recent times, been looked at by the Vatican, with the Pope speaking in the most forceful of language about the importance of reporting abuse and the protection of minors.

And, while the Church has never been a stranger to scandal, scandal always has an impact, and our response is crucial.

As members of the body of Christ, it is my belief that from the eucharistic table that we can regenerate and begin again.

It is through the sacraments, the cleansing that occurs in each, and the ongoing the renewal of baptismal promises that we can recommit ourselves to move forward.

Chapter Four
The Name of God Is Mercy

By welcoming a marginalized person whose body is wounded and by welcoming the sinner whose soul is wounded, we put our credibility as Christians on the line. Let us always remember the words of Saint John of the Cross: 'In the evening of life, we will be judged on love alone.'[1]

In 2018, the film *I Can Only Imagine*,[2] a movie that tells the story of Bart Millard, the composer of the song of the same name, hit cinemas across the country.

The song is based on Millard's own experience of growing up with an abusive, alcoholic father.

Millard has a conversion at a young age when attending a youth camp at his local Baptist Church, but even after this, continues to experience horrific abuse at the hands of his father until he finally leaves home.

He travels around with his Christian band (*Mercy Me*) for several years until he is prompted to return home. When he returns, he realises that not only is his father dying of pancreatic cancer, but that he has undergone a complete 180° conversion.

The last months they spend together are moments of joy and rebuilding of their relationship.

It's not easy for Millard to forgive his father, and he almost chooses to walk away but, by staying, he frees not only his father from racking guilt but liberates his own heart in the process.

---

1. Pope Francis, interview with Andrea Tornielli, translated by Oonagh Stransky, *The Name of God Is Mercy: A Conversation with Andrea Tornielli* (London: Bluebird Books for Life, 2014), 99.
2. Bart Millard, *I Can Only Imagine* (Santa Monica, Lionsgate, 2018).

As Millard farewells his father, he struggles through all the stages of grief, and as he does so, puts on paper his feelings. The song, 'I Can Only Imagine',[3] went on to be one of the best-selling singles of all time. Its theme is mercy and forgiveness.

This is what our Church is crying out for and we are not there yet. In Australia, we have a situation where people have suffered unimaginable crimes at the hands of priests and religious, and for many, there is simply too much to forgive.

In 2015, Pope Francis called an Extraordinary Jubilee of Mercy for the Church. Part of the reason for this was because of his specific heart for the poor and marginalised, part was due to his lifelong experience of God's merciful hand, and, perhaps most importantly, it was also because he saw a deep need in the Church to atone for its own sin, and to proclaim anew a story of mercy.

In doing this, Pope Francis proclaimed to us once again his utter faith in the person of Jesus Christ who so loved the world that he gave his life on the cross.

In choosing his papal motto, Pope Francis could have focused on any number of themes, but he chose '*miserando atque eligendo*', which doesn't have an exact translation in English but, loosely translated, means 'one who has been chosen and looked upon with mercy'.

Pope Francis does not exclude himself from the communion of sinners that make up our church, but rather places himself decidedly amid it. In doing so, he gives us hope.

By calling a Year of Mercy, he placed a focus on the most appealing image of God—a God who reaches down and wipes our tears away.

For some of us, we can find examples of God's mercy in stories from scripture. The New Testament abounds with stories such as the woman caught in adultery ('Go and sin no more', Jn 8:1–11); the prodigal son (who is welcomed back into the father's arms, Lk 15:11–32), and the woman who anoints Jesus at Bethany (those who have been forgiven much will have greater love, Jn 12:1–8).

One of my own favourites is the story of the Good Shepherd. I've been blessed to be surrounded by enough mercifully minded Catholics—clergy, religious and lay—who have been able to model to me the idea of being a Good Shepherd.

---

3. Bart Millard and Mercy Me, 'I Can Only Imagine' in *The Worship Project* (USA: Mercy Me, 1999).

When I have engaged with the style of prayer known as Imaginative Contemplation, I've often placed myself in the role of the lost sheep.

There's something quite powerful about imagining myself as a mangy, dirty and wild looking sheep, wandering aimless in the wilderness, and needing someone to bring me back to the fold.

In the distance, I see Jesus who has left the ninety-nine others to rescue me. I bound toward him, moved to tears, and imagine myself scooped up into his arms. And there is that moment of pure love.

This contemplation still has the capacity to move me to tears.

Pope Francis, in 2013, called upon ministers of the Gospel and pastors in the Church to have 'the smell of the sheep'. It is an enduring image.

He is calling the Church's leaders, and each of us too, to bend down and get dirty—to immerse ourselves in acts of mercy and justice.

But are we a church of mercy? In this chapter, I want to look at that, because I think we don't always communicate this well.

We prioritise our own comfort over that of others. We are intolerant, selfish, racist.

We don't allow that person to sit in OUR seat at the church.

We don't allow that person to sing in the choir.

We grumble at the person who comes for confession outside the marked times or prays a little too vocally as we sit in silence.

It was as a young person of twenty-two that I started to battle with the need *to do something*, to start living a more Christian vocation. My response was to sign up and volunteer overseas, and I was given the opportunity to work with the Jesuit Refugee Service for three months.

I arrived in Phnom Penh, Cambodia armed with a journalism degree, a year's worth of menial editing experience under my belt, and a guitar.

I felt like I had nothing really to give or do that would make much difference. At the same time, as a passionate photographer, I was questioning myself about photos—in particular, the taking of them.

In Cambodia, I saw more suffering than I had ever seen in my short life—those who had been maimed or incapacitated by landmines, refugees fleeing terror, beggars on the streets.

My friend, a Jesuit scholastic at the time who had also worked in this country was aware of my scrupulosity.

I had been afraid to take photos.

I didn't want to exploit anyone or steal their moment.

Gifted with an insight that was so simple and forthright, he asked me: 'Why don't you just ask them if you can take their picture? The worst they can do is say no.'

It was good advice. In doing so, it then allowed me to have some dialogue with people and to find out if I could do anything for their individual needs as well.

Even better advice came when I asked my friend about the feeling of uselessness. I couldn't speak more than a few words of Khmer, and my English lessons in the refugee camps were being met with mostly blank stares.

I was wondering if I had made the wrong decision. I wanted to be a Catholic missionary who changed the world one photograph and one English class at a time, but I wasn't making much progress.

As I shared all of this with him, he spoke some words from the spiritual exercises of St Ignatius: 'Beth, the best thing you can do is ask yourself these questions: How can I be the image of Christ to this person? How can I best show that?'

In fact, it is at the end of one of the meditations in *The Spiritual Exercises of Saint Ignatius* that we are asked three questions: 'What have I done for Christ?', 'What am I doing for Christ?' and 'What will I do for Christ?'[4]

From then on, I could more actively (although still with some scrupulosity) test my actions and responses in the light of these questions, and more and more, the faces of these people would enter my prayer.

At the time of writing this chapter, I found myself attending Mass when the Gospel for the day was Mark 1:40–55, where Jesus has compassion on the leper who comes, asking to be healed.

The Greek word for compassion means to 'feel from one's guts'.

The priest explained that feeling, that moment we have when we absolutely must reach out, where we are physically moved to action.

For me, that gut-feeling often comes when I review a social media feed and see images of rescue animals, or when I see some child washing windscreens in the streets of a Latin American capital.

---

4. Saint Ignatius of Loyola, and Thomas Corbishley, *The Spiritual Exercises of Saint Ignatius of Loyola* (Mineola, NY: Dover Publications, 2011).

At other moments it's seeing a homeless man and his dog on the streets on my own city, battling the elements. And what is my response?

What it comes down to is a choice. Often, we are so moved with compassion that merciful actions simply flow from us, and we can alleviate suffering in some way, however small.

Now, of course, it's clear that we cannot do everything, we cannot respond to every need or be everything to all people, but we can't just do nothing either.

We need to seek a balance. We can't be a Good Samaritan on every street corner, bathing the wounds of the most downtrodden with oil and paying in advance for their lodgings.

Many challenged even Mother Teresa on her preference to directly seek out people and care for them, often without an explicit advocacy or justice element.

I would argue that we need both. We need the individual charitable response that is born out of our commitment to mercy, and we need social justice advocacy—there is a time for each.

Ultimately, in these situations where we are confronted on street corners and our compassion is challenged, we do well to reach out in conversation and engage in dialogue where time permits.

Sometimes, the balm of mercy could come in the form of a muesli bar and a bottle of water. Other times it could be accompanying the person to a hostel for a warm bed for the night. Then there are times when these responses might be deeply patronising. It always needs to be a dialogue. Often the most charitable thing is to simply listen and acknowledge that, while you can't do everything, you have recognised one another's humanity.

'You will always have the poor with you', said Jesus. And if in those moments where we are confronted with these very human situations, perhaps the best question we can ask is: 'How can I, within my modern-day context, be the face of Christ to this person?'

This action on its own will respond to Pope Francis' ideal of making the world (and indeed the Church) a little less cold.

And, while on the subject of Pope Francis, it's worth looking at the unique gifts he has brought to the Church since his election in 2013. Pope Francis' way of proceeding has baffled, inspired, and challenged us to move beyond our comfortable Christianity.

There are some that grapple with him, not the least of whom are prelates and clerics, princes of the Church. Significant efforts have been made to dismantle him, even at a curial level.

But even Jesus says to us that a prophet isn't welcome in their own hometown (Lk 4:16–30).

I think perhaps this prophet is not welcomed by all because he makes them uncomfortable.

Look at his early actions: washing the feet of women and Muslims and prisoners; travelling to Lampedusa to be with refugees from North Africa; riding on the bus to his lodgings with the other cardinals after being elected. Each is a small but symbolic act.

To me, Pope Francis has not only been a breath of fresh air for the Church, but who, more than any other Pope in history (to my knowledge), has been so open about his own personal sinfulness that he has evangelised by his very frailty.

He hasn't in this sense become a relativist about our sinfulness as some might suggest, but he has led us to better understand God's infinite mercy, he has pointed to a God who never gets tired of showing mercy.

In an unprecedented interview with Jesuit Fr Antonio Spadaro SJ, which went on to be published in English as 'A Big Heart Open to God',[5] Pope Francis spoke for the first time about his life, in a way no other Pope had before.

His courage in facing up to possible scrutiny (and plenty of people criticised him for his openness and humility) showed a person of discernment, who sought the greater good—and in this case, it was opening to the world and to God.

Pope Francis, or rather, Jorge Mario Bergoglio, went to Rome without the expectation of being elected. Even in the days before the conclave he could walk incognito around the streets of Rome with barely any recognition from journalists.

Other names were being touted as 'papabile' (those cardinals who might possibly be elected), but he appeared on few lists, even though he had been the dark horse in the 2005 conclave which elected Pope Benedict.

---

5. Pope Francis, interviewed by Antonio Spadaro, 'A Big Heart Open to God: An Interview with Pope Francis', *America*, 30 September 2013 at <https://www.americamagazine.org/faith/2013/09/30/big-heart-open-god-interview-pope-francis>. Accessed 9 September 2019.

It is told that he chose the name Francis for the poor and was inspired to do so when his friend Cláudio Cardinal Hummes of Brazil lent over to him on his election and whispered: 'Don't forget about the poor.'

It is unlikely that the Pope, who had spent so much time in the *villas miseria* (misery villages), the slums of Buenos Aires, would have forgotten about the poor, but we can all be corrupted by comfort and power.

Very quickly, images and stories emerged of him paying his hotel bill, phoning his friends, cancelling his newspaper subscription, kissing the lepers of society in often moving scenes.

We don't always however, as Catholics, show this same type of mercy. We don't always invite others to the banquet. While it is easy to point to the fact that in the Catholic church, those of other faiths and none are not able to receive communion, we should not forget to look at the soup kitchens, and refugee welcome centres, and homeless shelters to name just a few that invite all who hunger and thirst for righteousness.

It is challenging though, when there are moments which at first sight may seem like exclusion, but one of the outstanding characteristics of Pope Francis' dialogue with those of other faiths has been his language and gestures of welcome.

He is open about not always getting it right.

What Pope Francis has shown us in his public persona, and in stories about his more private actions—including many lifesaving ones during the military dictatorship in Argentina—is that he is a man of courage, who genuinely seeks Jesus as his ultimate model, guide and saviour.

I would like to see him continue to emphasise that, pointing first of all to Jesus, but also reminding us, as he has so effectively done thus far that we all matter and belong to the people of God, the communion of saints, the cloud of witnesses, and that we are all invited to that banquet, and are all called to renew and transform this Church with love.

Chapter Five
Women Who Follow Jesus

One needn't identify as a feminist to participate in the redemptive movement of God for women in the world, the Gospel is more than enough. Of course, it is! But as long as I know how important maternal health is to Haiti's future, and as long as I know that women are being abused and raped, as long as I know girls are being denied life itself through selective abortion, abandonment, and abuse, as long as brave little girls in Afghanistan are attacked with acid for the crime of going to school, and until being a Christian is synonymous with doing something about these things, you can also call me a feminist.[1]

There are all kinds of anecdotes that religious sisters and priests will tell about the women in their lives. Most will say that the reason they have remained in the Church, or at the very least, people of faith, has been because of the nurturing on the part of their mothers.

And yet, the role of women in the Church is one of the hot-button issues that I have confronted again and again throughout my life.

My first encounter was in third grade, when I boldly approached my parish priest, a good man, a man who would spend hours on a Saturday night after dinner discussing theology with my parents over a shared meal at our house. On this day, I asked if I could be trained as an altar server.

The uncomfortable, 'oh, well, we don't really do that here' was not met with anger from myself. I rather felt sorry for him that he was unable to explain why, in our parish, girls couldn't serve on the altar and that in the neighbouring parish, most of the altar servers were girls.

---

1. Sarah Bessey, *Jesus Feminist: An Invitation to Revisit the Bible's View of Women: Exploring God's Radical Notion That Women Are People, Too* (Nashville: Howard Books, 2013), 171–172.

My survey respondents felt the same. Here is a sample of their often-frustrated responses to the question 'How do you feel about the place of women in the Church?'

> *It's like slavery: they [women] do so much and it's taken for granted and [they] are treated like idiots, incapable of leadership. They are the natural source of pastoral direction.*

> *I think it's ridiculous that women cannot be priests or deacons. I think the Church's arguments against these practices are shameless in their demand that we put aside scripture, theology and common sense. A perfect example of the abuse of power in the church.*

> *Women are essential in the Church, so too are leaders. We need more courageous, progressive and valiant women to speak out for truth, justice. Cannot have a whole without two halves (the balance of both the feminine and the masculine).*

> *The Church needs to formally acknowledge the work that is already being done by women—women deacons are a no-brainer. The Church should be a leader in having women as leaders. They've got a long way to go, and they need to get going. A woman in every Curial department. A woman in every part of the governance structure, and men who are qualified for the roles they are allocated to who are directed to employ qualified women. The list is endless. Women are equal in the eyes of God, so the Catholic Church needs to catch up and follow the lead of Jesus. Instead, they are perpetuating stereotypes in many places, especially in developing nations.*

In my case, I look to the women who have nurtured my faith. While my father attended church and was an active Vincentian, it was my mother who was the catechist, the lead parent, the evangeliser, the pray-er, the one who woke up in the middle of the night to tend to us, and perhaps even sing a lullaby that down the track we would realise had been taken from the words of scripture.

The story of women as teachers of the faith is clear. They were among the very first catechists, the first builders of the Early Church. They were first ones to proclaim the paschal mystery.

They went to the empty tomb and met the Lord after the Resurrection. It was the women who had the courage to stay at the foot of the cross.

Yet we still find ourselves relegated to the kitchen for the potluck dinner, not worthy to celebrate the heavenly meal perhaps, but quite good enough to clean the dishes.

St Catherine of Siena is famously quoted as saying: 'Be who you were created to be, and you will set the world on fire.'

Born in 1347, St Catherine no doubt was asked to cook, clean, and perhaps iron more than one altar cloth. She also told the Pope of the time to 'man up' and get himself back to Rome and stand up to his Cardinals.

She set the world on fire, even as an illiterate woman who had to dictate her writings to others. She was the first female Doctor of the Church.

The second female doctor, St Teresa of Avila, frustrated at many of the things she was unable to do due to her gender, is quoted as saying: 'Being a woman in this Church is enough to make my wings fall off.' Despite this, she spread her wings and reformed the Carmelites, so imagine what we can do, despite adversity, 500 years on.

This chapter in many ways is the hardest for me to write. Many of the greatest struggles I have with my dear mother Church are associated with some of my experiences as a young woman.

One of the things I keep reminding myself of, however, is the prominence of women in the Gospels. I think of the passage from Isaiah that informs Mary's Magnificat, recorded in Luke's Gospel.

The beauty of the Magnificat is the idea of women—and in this context, Mary—rejoicing in being image bearers of God.

But it would be fair to say that, at times in the Church, women do not feel as though they are image-bearers.

Almost twenty years ago, the largest research project ever undertaken by the Australian Catholic Bishops Conference (ACBC) was *Woman and Man: One in Christ Jesus*. It's a heavy tome, about the size of a Bible. Its findings show that women's participation is crucial to the survival of the Church.

The report found:

> The dominant issue arising from the research was gender equality. It recognised the equal dignity of women and

men created in the image and likeness of God, but that the Church was seen to be lagging the wider Australian society in recognising the changing role of women as one of the 'signs of the times' and affirming the equality of women. The very limited participation of women in decision-making at present and the need to increase women's involvement in decision-making at all levels were constant and major themes.[2]

According to the most recent National Church Life Survey results, women make up more than 66 per cent of Catholics in this country.

Some women in the church that I've spoken to feel overworked and underpaid. Some feel quite content with their various ministries and involvement. Some seek to be better included in councils and decision-making bodies, and others feel called to ministries that are off limits to them.

Some dioceses are responding well to this challenge.

> *I think that work is already being done to address what can be addressed in the current situation. Many bishops are appointing qualified women to leadership roles in their dioceses/ archdioceses and this is making a difference. Some parishes who have acolytes are now either appointing or considering appointing women to such roles as seeing women 'up there on the altar' is a start in changing the consciousness of both clergy and laity. I have found being on key women's committees is useful—if nothing else it opens up opportunities to meet other like-minded people. Having 'named' roles at parish level that women can undertake is a way to go.* (Survey respondent)

However, it can be tricky. Even at a diocesan level there is a limit to how much can be done without support from the institutional Church. In theory, women can do anything in the Church, apart from seeking priestly ministry.

There have been conversations more recently about restoring the office of deacon to women, of which there is much evidence in the Early Church, but the flow-down effects of this can be far more exclusionary than the lack of opportunity to be a priest on its own.

---

2. Committee for Justice, Development and Peace, *Woman and Man: One in Christ Jesus: Report on the Participation of Women in the Catholic Church in Australia* (Sydney, NSW: HarperCollinsReligious, 1999), vii.

An ABC Religion reporter and theologian using social media in 2018, weighed into the debate on women deacons with the following comment:

Romans, verses 16:1–2 indicates deacon Phoebe—who was recommended by St Paul (1 Tim 3:11)—also refers to women deacons in the early church: 'In the same way, the women are to be worthy of respect, not malicious talkers but temperate and trustworthy in everything.' That is to say, in so far as any male was ordained a deacon, the same applied to females. And maybe even not either of them 'ordained' in the modern sense. Plain scripture. (Noel Debien, 2019.)

There are several examples I wish to share here, that show some level of systematic exclusion of women.

In the early 1900s, women were not allowed to sing in church choirs. Now, some of our best liturgical composers are women.

As mentioned earlier, when I received my first communion, our parish priest said 'no' to female altar servers, despite other parishes in the archdiocese being open to the possibility. Now, female servers are a common sight across the world, although this practice is not universally accepted.

Women still find meaning in this faith; across the world they are represented in much greater numbers than men.

My mother finds meaning in her faith as she plays tambourine in the Saturday night folk choir.

My friend Maria is the president of a local St Vincent de Paul conference and lives her faith out in action; my friend Annie directs a diocesan communications office.

We are teachers, lawyers, agency heads, psychologists, doctors, stay-at-home mums.

We are pastoral associates, prophets, and even princesses, claimed one friend. She was initially being flippant, but as one who is theologically trained, she started wondering about the fact that if men could be cardinals, and thus 'princes' of the Church, maybe women could be princesses? After all, the office of Cardinal does not actually require ordination.

This woman was known to an Australian prelate, famous for a doctrinarian approach to pastoral matters. When he saw her at a meeting, he smiled as they greeted one another and quipped: 'Hello, Princess.' Word does get around.

I suspect that the reason my Grandmother, born an Anglican, converted after having six children had much to do with the fact that the Anglican Church seemed slightly more progressive than the faith in which her children were being raised.

She used to giggle at the story of my aunt coming home from catechism class saying: 'Don't worry mum, God will forgive you for not being a Catholic.'

Yet, as she went to her eternal reward in 2014, she had her rosary beads and a palm cross from Indonesia close by her side.

I have never had much of a Marian devotion, but it was through pondering Mary's courage and her 'yes' that I started to see some innate value in learning more about her, and I started to think of the radical leadership of the Church embodied by Mary.

I began to realise what a complete powerhouse Mary was and is for us. We have a Church, that for all its clericalism and hierarchy, has a woman who is more important than all the popes, princes and priests of the Church.

Of course, the challenge often is looking beyond or past the leadership and making peace with the fact that most of that leadership still struggles to work out what the place of women is.

A friend of mine has a PhD in Catholic Social Teaching, and in the early 2000s was appointed to the directorship of a Church agency.

A significant post in the Church, the bishops would have been kept abreast of this development, and would have known about her, particularly considering she would be representing them on key issues of justice.

Nonetheless, as she arrived for her first meeting with them, she was mistaken for one of the hospitality staff, and asked by a bishop if she would make him a cup of tea. Over a decade later, I had a similar moment when a seminary rector recognised me in a similar situation.

'Oh, Beth! Lovely to see you! Are you here doing some typing for the bishops?', he enquired, smiling. He is now a senior church official in a diocese, and again, not a bad person.

While Pope Francis has affirmed John Paul II's letter *Ordinatio Sacerdotalis* (which affirmed that priestly ordination was restricted to men alone) and has said that the door is closed to women's ordination in the Church, he has spoken about the need for more women's leadership and for a definitive theology of women to be developed and integrated into the life of the Church.

From this, we are perhaps to understand that often when God closes a door, God opens a window somewhere, and this enables us to have the freedom to choose not to embrace some of the negative aspects that ordination and a clerical culture in the Church have caused and embodied, and to bring about a new form of positive leadership.

While there absolutely needs to be an ongoing dialogue about how women's gifts can be better used in Church leadership, there are still some very specific ways that we can already transform the Church.

In truth, it is likely that real renewal of the Catholic Church will only ever be possible if women's gifts are given more prominence, in whatever form that might take. Already, women across the world preach and proselytise, care and nurture, create and enunciate the power of the Church in our lives—a Church that is teacher, nurturer, prophet, mother, and womb.

Chapter Six
Education in the Catholic Tradition

An education in the fullness of humanity should be the defining feature of Catholic schools.[1]

Pope Francis (2015)

Catholic schools, in theory, should be charged with bringing about the Kingdom of God on earth, to proclaim the truth, beauty and goodness of our faith in a holistic way.

'An education in the fullness of humanity should be the defining feature of Catholic schools', said Pope Francis when speaking in 2015 to members of the Association of Catholic School Parents in Italy.

'Speaking about a Catholic education is equivalent to speaking about the human, about humanism', he said.

'An inclusive education finds a place for all and does not select in an elitist way the beneficiaries of its efforts.'

The Catholic education system in Australia is one of the beacons of light in our Church, and when done well, can pave the way to an extraordinary future.

At the same time, Catholic education has also been at the centre of funding debates, and many practising Catholics argue the toss about whether schools really are evangelising young people.

I have a mixed view of this, and no two schools are the same, just as no two teachers are the same. That said, if a school embraces a

---

1. Pope Francis, 'Address of His Holiness Pope Francis to the Association of Catholic School Parents (AGESC)' at <https://w2.vatican.va/content/francesco/en/speeches/2015/december/documents/papa-francesco_20151205_agesc.html.> Accessed 27 September 2019.

holistic Christianity, its people can be hopeful witnesses to the 'good news' of the Gospel and the tradition.

Of course, in an ever-changing culture, and conscious of the decline in practice of faith, even in Catholic schools there is no guarantee that those employed to teach religion necessarily practice, and/or, have a true understanding of the faith they are teaching.

The deposit of faith, the *kerygma*, is indeed a gift, and not one that all Catholic school teachers possess. Education theorist Richard Rymarz writes that the discussion of Catholic schools as centres of the New Evangelisation can be a difficult one. Rymarz and others are right to suggest that it cannot necessarily be assumed that Catholic teachers are joyful witnesses of that faith they supposedly have.

Very often, however, for various reasons, Religious Education is not necessarily viewed as an important subject.

Teachers and students alike often see what is problematic in the institutional Church instead of what is beautiful about a life lived with faith.

Indeed, some Catholic schools across Australia have removed Religious Education as a compulsory subject, which is not only a defeatist approach, but can very quickly impact on the culture of the school.

Anecdotally, many teachers who are employed in the Catholic Education system feel that it less and less resonates with their own beliefs. In addition to this, the resourcing for teachers in such an important subject is crucial to the transmission of the Gospel. Maurice Ryan and Patricia Malone in their 2003 text *Exploring the Religion Classroom: A Guidebook for Catholic Schools* write on how important it is to create resources for teaching and transmitting faith.

> It is necessary to develop teaching and learning processes that assist students to understand and appreciate the richness of the tradition in ways that allow them to question and probe in order to find sources of new understandings.[2]

John McGrath of the Broken Bay Institute argued about the importance of culture in schools in 2014 in a journal article titled 'Possibili-

---

2. Maurice Ryan and Patricia Malone, *Exploring the Religion Classroom: A Guidebook for Catholic Schools* (Wentworth Falls, NSW: Social Science Press, 1996)

ties for New Evangelisation of Catholic School Students, Teachers and Parents'.³ He suggested that the entire culture of a Catholic school, not just subject-based instruction on religion can have an impact on evangelisation, and if then there is an explicit link made across the institution between culture, charism and the 'why', that is, the mission of Jesus.

> The most significant forces for new evangelisation are the Catholic character of a school, its charism, culture, relationships and quality of pastoral care, all explicitly motivated by relationship with Jesus. If they are only implicitly Catholic, diminished or absent, a school's capacity for new evangelisation will be much reduced. The prayer life of the school is another key aspect.⁴

Catholic Education has changed significantly in this country and worldwide. That said, some history is worth considering.

My parents were educated in an era of fierce nuns and brothers in schools run almost exclusively by religious. There was regular use of corporal punishment and a general atmosphere of rote learning rather than education that would lead to people who knew how to think.

More than fifty years later, my dad still tells stories about the difficult Christian Brother who provoked an early end to his Catholic education.

Even now, every time I head off on retreat, my father calls me 'Sister Sebastian', clearly a nun who had a negative and lasting impression on him when he attended Catholic primary school in Ballarat.

Over the last twenty years, it has been near impossible for me to attend any kind of faith-based retreat without him making a joke of it. He quips that while I say I am going on a prayer retreat, in truth, I am in fact most likely on my way to a 'strap-making course', to learn how to 'soak them in vinegar for ultimate efficacy'.

---

3. John McGrath, 'Possibilities for New Evangelisation of Catholic School Students, Teachers and Parents', in *Journal of Religious Education*. 62 (2014): 15–24 at <https://doi.org/10.1007/s40839-014-0002-5>. Accessed 9 September 2019.
4. McGrath, 'Possibilities for New Evangelisation of Catholic School Students, Teachers and Parents'

Such are some of the difficult experiences that have journeyed with him throughout his life and challenged his faith.

Corporal punishment is long gone from Catholic schools in this country, but for some, it has left physical and emotional scars.

By the 1990s, things had changed. None of my teachers in Catholic school were nuns or brothers, and that is the experience for most young people today.

As a teacher now in a Catholic school and having watched the impact of Catholic education in several countries, I am starting to learn much more about how beautiful a legacy a decent Catholic education can be, but equally how damaging a poor one can be.

Here are some reflections on different Catholic educational models which seem to be best practice, and some stories about my own journey through Catholic schools, as both student and teacher.

On the day of my Confirmation in 1994, there was excitement in the air. I had a new outfit—a ruffled white shirt and beige pants. I had a cute little vest to go with it and new shoes. I was thrilled to have chosen my own colours, remembering back to three years earlier as we painstakingly tried on hundreds of pairs of white satin shoes for my First Communion.

Confirmation was different. At twelve, I got to choose my own outfit, and there was no fluffy white dress required.

Instead, the symbolism of the sacrament would be demonstrated by a red silk sash which, from memory, bore the white cut-out shape of a dove, to represent the Holy Spirit.

My parents used to make a big deal of our sacraments, putting on a family lunch and taking lots of photos.

Our Godparents and extended family would be invited for roast lamb and I remember receiving all manner of religious gifts that would then be relegated to a top shelf and untouched until I was eighteen.

These gifts included a Bible and some rosary beads. Also, and more memorable at the time, was an image of Mary in blown glass given to me by my music teacher, a lapsed Catholic. All now take pride of place in my bookcase at home.

The Church where I made my Confirmation was typical of 1980s architecture—a brick, A-frame building. Friends would later refer to it as 'the beige church'.

It would be fair to say we were underprepared for Confirmation. We had one in-service day where we had been taken through the physical instructions, and being slightly asthmatic, I had missed that day.

My catechist mother came to the rescue and I was shown where to stand as Bishop Pat Power announced the name 'St Thérèse of the Child Jesus' and laid his hands on my head.

Year Six, my final year of primary school, was my last year of Catholic schooling and it was a mixed experience.

I flourished in the religious diversity of the government education system during my high school years, but I graduated with the sense that I had missed something.

I would find myself playing Trivial Pursuit with another friend from a Catholic family and was embarrassed that I knew few of the answers to the questions about the Bible, even though we went to church each Sunday, rain, hail or shine.

Some may dismiss the stories that appear again and again in the religious education curriculum as too pedestrian, but in fact, stories such as the Good Samaritan, the Beatitudes, the Prodigal Son, and the Woman with the Alabaster Jar are just a few of the stories with profound messages that get a run across grade levels, and with good reason. Each of these is a story that quite specifically shows the character of God. These stories are then given flesh and find expression in classes as varied as Ethics, the Search for Meaning, Philosophy, Psychology and Comparative Religion.

It's not only learning the Gospel stories from Jesus' time, but those stories of the saints and sinners across the centuries, and the way they integrate their faith into solid, compassionate and holistic values that are the best legacy of this education system.

In 2007, many years after Confirmation and with my Catholic schooling long since finished, I developed a strong interest in my faith. It had become central to my life. A seed had been planted in my primary school years and, by a regular practice of faith, I was beginning to integrate it into my own existence.

There was something tugging at my heart, and my fascination would eventually lead me down the path of apostolic religious communities of women. Coupled with this were the ministries they were involved in, which almost always included education.

By 2007, I'd done some postgraduate study in theology, journalism and editing, as well as a short course on interfaith relations.

A study of pedagogy or education was what was missing, and I felt a yearning to start learning about how I might impart knowledge in a classroom.

At the time, I had a strong feeling that I wanted to do some volunteer work overseas in an educational context, and inevitably, as I contacted different groups, or found different ministries that I might volunteer with, a name kept popping up. Fe y Alegría. The name on its own was enough to provoke my interest. Faith and Joy.

Fe y Alegría is a movement for integrated development education and was founded in Venezuela in the 1950s by Fr José María Vélaz SJ, and today its network has schools across every Latin American country.

Their motto is 'Where the road stops (or where the asphalt stops) Fe y Alegría begins'.

Their mission is to go to the poorest, most under-resourced communities, and provide a holistic Catholic education, grounded in values of development, and informed by the local culture.

As my search continued, I realised that this movement was responsible for educating millions of the poorest children in South America.

And so it was that in 2008, I found myself working at one of those schools in the dusty, marginalised barrio of Bañado Norte, in Asuncion, Paraguay. Years later when I would spend a year there, I would understand in a deep way why this community's name is literally 'The Northern Bath'. The place is dusty and dry for most of the year, but when it rains, it pours.

The intense flooding happens quickly and forces people into makeshift shelters constructed from whatever thin wood they can get their hands on. Even amid such flooding, the dedicated teachers continued their mission to serve and educate. Classes happened side by side with common pot meals, and when nothing seemed to function properly, and nobody had a secure place to call home, the school became their home.

I observed how the teachers would stay back long into the night. The director of the college would get on a bus at 4:30am and arrive at the college between 6:30 and 7.00 in the morning, after walking a three kilometre stretch of dirt road.

The little school, called *Ca'acupemi*, named after a Paraguayan apparition, was home to 200 students, and, when the rain came, all their homes would be under water.

Yet, the education continued, and when the school day finished, the teachers would get together to prepare meals. They coped with the extraordinary chaos caused by the flooding and were strengthened by an enduring sense of faith and joy during struggle, buoyed by a mission to love and serve the most vulnerable.

This educational model is just one example of how Catholic Social Teaching values have been integrated deeply into parts of Latin American culture so that a multitude of people can receive a free, high-quality education focused on the holistic development of the human person.

In the United States, partly inspired by the work of Fe y Alegría and Fr Vélaz, but also wanting to adapt to the urban poverty present in cities like Chicago, Cristo Rey (Christ the King) was founded. Cristo Rey schools, now numbering thirty-two, are Catholic education and Ignatian ingenuity and collaboration at their best.

Cristo Rey has a unique program of seeking out students from families who are unable to pay private school fees, and integrating a work and study program. Effectively, students, a large proportion from Latino or African American backgrounds, spend up to two days working in corporate offices, offices which in turn pay a low-level salary to cover students' tuition costs. Students then do longer hours at school on the days that they attend.

Closer to home is the story of Gemma Sisia, an Australian woman from Armidale who, along with many volunteers, has founded the 2,000 strong School of St Jude in Arusha, Tanzania. The school only welcomes students who live in abject poverty and ensures that each child gets the best education available in the entire country.

And, of course, how could I fail to mention St Mary of the Cross MacKillop, Australia's first saint, who founded the first free Catholic school in Australia in 1866 and remained dedicated to serving the poorest children in this country until her death.

Across the world, there are many examples like this. It would be impossible to share all the incredible stories of how Catholic education is changing the lives of people far beyond the walls of churches.

These days, Catholic schools are likely to have students of all faiths and none, but rather than hinder the work, this adds to its richness.

Perhaps there is a sense of needing to work to the future and plant seeds. Implicit in this mission is the sharing of the beauty of our tradition.

Chapter Seven
The Parish Community

The parish is the presence of the Church in a given territory, an environment for hearing God's word, for growth in the Christian life, for dialogue, proclamation, charitable outreach, worship and celebration. In all its activities the parish encourages and trains its members to be evangelisers. It is a community of communities, a sanctuary where the thirsty come to drink amid their journey, and a centre of constant missionary outreach. We must admit, though, that the call to review and renew our parishes has not yet sufficed to bring them nearer to people, to make them environments of living communion and participation, and to make them completely mission-oriented.[1]

The Catholic parish is very much the face of the Church. It is the place where most of the sacraments are administered.

It is where pastoral care happens.

It is where, in theory and often in practice, we gather each week to celebrate.

There are tears of joy and of sorrow, weddings, funerals, baptisms, confirmations, liturgies, masses, shared daily eucharist, fellowship, cups of coffee, reconciliation and much more.

The parish is the hub of Catholicism and can have an enormous impact on whether people stay or go.

---

1. Pope Francis, *Evangelii Gaudium: Apostolic Exhortation on the Proclamation of the Gospel in Today's World* (24 November 2013) at <http://w2.vatican.va/content/francesco/en/apost_exhortations/documents/papa-francesco_esortazione-ap_20131124_evangelii-gaudium.html>. Accessed 9 September 2019.

For you, however, the local parish might be the source of all boredom.

Perhaps you have a priest who has lost his vigour, a choir that sounds like it's strangling a cat, and parishioners with personalities that resemble blocks of wood.

Most of us in ordinary Australian parish land rarely have that sense of the transcendent. In fact, perhaps the more we attend mass, the less we are inclined to experience it.

Often, we are tired, lukewarm and attending simply out of a sense of obligation. This is of course a two-sided problem. Parishes do need to make more effort in areas such as welcome, liturgy, music, preaching and community, but sometimes we, too, need to ask what we are bringing to the proverbial table. Involvement in parish can often make all the difference.

As I was writing this book, I had been to six parishes in as many weeks, most of which were not my local parish community. For various reasons, I had been giving talks, volunteering, providing music ministry or attending events.

It was a jarring experience because most of the moments spent in those churches were ones of frustration. Not being greeted, people turning away during the sign of peace, priests who in some cases had such poor English that even the known parts of the mass couldn't be understood.

I didn't feel connected until I landed upon a former parish where I had spent years playing music—a vibrant parish which was the result of a successful amalgamation and which had standing room only.

The archbishop was initiating a new parish priest, and the community was cohesive and warm. There were smiles of recognition and a cup of tea after mass, so much so that the longer length of the mass had made no difference to my desire to be there.

In the book *Rebuilt: The Story of a Catholic Parish*,[2] Fr Michael White and Tom Corcoran recount how they transformed a fledgling parish in Baltimore into a hub of activity, a place of transformation, by praying with the parishioners, trying new things and discerning how they could best be the body of Christ in suburban USA.

---

2. Michael White, and Tom Corcoran, *Rebuilt: The Story of a Catholic Parish: Awakening the Faithful, Reaching the Lost, Making Church Matter* (Notre Dame, Ind: Ave Maria Press, 2013).

While many of the things they did would never work in Australian parishes, there is much to learn from their techniques. The main message was that they returned wholeheartedly to the Gospels and asked what a parish should look like. They visited evangelical megachurches in the area to learn what worked, and how it was that people could become connected again.

The description of the book reads as follows:

> Our parish wasn't working, said the leaders of a Catholic church in Maryland. We didn't know how to fix it. We can learn from churches that are getting it right. Drawing on the wisdom gleaned from thriving mega-churches and innovative business leaders while anchoring their vision in the Eucharistic centre of Catholic faith, Fr. Michael White and lay associate Tom Corcoran present the compelling and inspiring story to how they brought their parish back to life.[3]

Much of what they could do to transform their parish needs cultural nuance. Some of it would work in Australia, and other parts not so much. But adapting it to the local community has much to recommend it.

Parishes in Australia are emptying at a somewhat alarming rate.

In the United State, the fastest growing 'denomination' is ex-Catholics. According to Brandon Vogt's book *Why I Am Catholic (And You Should Be Too)*, for every six people that leave the Catholic Church, only one enters through Baptism or RCIA (Rite of Christian Initiation of Adults)[4] and so it is always a surprise when travelling to see places where the Church is not in decline. It still surprises me to see a full church anywhere in Australia unless there is some special occasion.

Some say that the answers to the future of the Church in places like Australia will be found in new movements, those with expressions of faith that appeal to people at different life stages, or those that enunciate a nuanced sense of spirituality.

Others say that the beauty is to be found in parishes that do things well.

---

3. White and Corcoran, *Rebuilt*
4. Vogt, *Why I Am Catholic (and You Should Be Too)*.

I interviewed one priest some years back about what it means to do parish well, and he was quite clear that there were four elements that made a big difference to whether a parish would thrive or not.

Preaching is important. People need to hear homilies and feel engaged by a priest; they need the Gospel to be made relevant to their day-to-day existence.

Music is important; when the music is not well done, it can often have the effect of turning people away.

Contemplation and silence are important, too. People need to feel that church is a place they can come to pray and experience the Lord. Our culture doesn't always allow for that.

And finally, welcome and community. In fact, perhaps that should be the first thing. Communion, feeling part of the body of Christ, is so important.

Dr Trudy Dantis, who currently heads up the Australian Church's Pastoral Research Office, undertook some ground-breaking research between 2008 and 2015 into factors that lead to parish vitality.

She did this to provide Australian case studies with down-to-earth examples of what can be achieved in eight key areas that lead to stronger parishes. These areas are planning, spirituality and faith formation, liturgy, community building, welcoming and hospitality, outreach, evangelisation and leadership.

In what became known as the 'Building Stronger Parishes' project, she brought together the experiences of people from across Australian parishes and profiled some best-practice examples.

In one of the preliminary reports which was released in 2012, Dr Dantis wrote about the best practice in various parishes the project team had visited across several rural and metropolitan dioceses around the country. One of those focused on was the rural parish of Shepparton in the Diocese of Sandhurst. In part, the report said:

> The commitment to welcoming is also evident in a number of ways, through the Faith and Light program for the disabled; the active St Vincent de Paul conference and the Bereavement group; the special Liturgical arrangements made for the Sudanese and Congolese parishioners; the deep involvement in the Inter-Church Council of the area; and in the long-standing ministry of visiting the sick and the elderly within the parish. The parish takes great care with its liturgies, ensuring they are at its heart. The emphasis on adult faith formation

and the scripture sessions run by the priests ensure there is an ongoing deepening of the gospel vision. This is the prime means of connecting up and grounding parishioners; and the rhythm of the liturgy—we are invited in so we may be sent out—is the rhythm of parish life.[5]

In this preliminary report, and in the final report that was released in book form in 2015, key themes such as welcome, commitment, service to the vulnerable, focus on liturgy and sending out tend to be enduring qualities of parishes that 'do it well', parishes that really seek to embody Gospel values.

Research does, however, show that most parishes don't always do all these things perfectly. Even in the *Building Stronger Parishes* report, the 'best practice' examples don't always have a one hundred per cent success rate in every area. And, the question needs to be asked, is the reason people attend church due to the experiences they have in a parish? For some this is true.

For others, it may be their experience of community through some of the new movements of the Church. While one person might find community and a sense of enlivenment in their faith by attending charismatic mass run by the Disciples of Jesus each week, others might prefer the monthly recollection offered by Opus Dei. Some like the family-based approach of the Neo-Catechumenal way; others again might like their local young adults' group which offers rosary and adoration, followed by pizza. A young man of twenty-two who responded to my survey said that he had found the most solace in attending the traditional Latin mass, and that, for him, it was a true expression of community.

Some people find that their extra time is best used in service-based ministries such as St Vincent de Paul, and that this brings them a sense of wholeness in their local parish. Others prefer a rosary group or preparing meals for the sick and housebound. Others find their deepest joy in involvement in the liturgy, through music or ministry of the word.

These different expressions within and in addition to the 'parish' are all valid and perhaps crucial to the survival of the Church in Australia.

---

5. ACBC Pastoral Research Office, *Building Stronger Parishes Preliminary Report: 2012 Supplement* at https://www.buildingstrongerparishes.catholic.org.au/pdf/BSP%20Prelim%20Report%202012%20Supplement.pdf>. Accessed 3 February 2020.

I began something of a pilgrimage around churches in our archdiocese during the writing of this book. I felt it was important to know what was going on more generally, instead of focusing on just a few examples.

There had been a lot of movement of priests as well as some amalgamations of parishes in recent years.

The particular parish I landed on in early January one year had purple carpet and wooden pews, with frayed copies of the green Catholic worship book placed in between the back rest and the kneeler.

The church was that A-frame shape that was prominent in the 1970s and 1980s. The stained-glass windows had bold shapes depicting what seemed a quite accurate image of Jesus, at least in this case he had darker skin than the pasty white Aryan we are used to in this part of the world.

Another window showed glass triangles in the form of red fire, a symbol of the Holy Spirit and, while beautiful, seemed to add to the heat of the summer day.

The mercury had reached 40°C, and I'd chosen this mass partly for the priest who had recently taken up residence there, and partly for the rumour that it was a drive-through mass.

As I reflected on that though, I realised how even I wanted to just tick it off, get it done, forgetting for a moment about the sacredness of it all.

It was then, and not a few more times in the course of my writing, that I realised what was most important for me when choosing a mass. To me, it was a community. The choice of mass that day was largely because I would catch up with the priest, who is also a friend, after mass.

Community rated highly when I interviewed people about what keeps them united with the Church—it was the second highest answer after the Eucharist. A parish community can be the difference between whether someone stays in the institution or not.

Ultimately, if the parish is to be the best version of itself, and thus be a more positive space where most of the evangelical activity of the Church takes place, then it needs to heed what people are saying.

While some people who vote with their feet leave for larger, institutional reasons, if they have had a positive experience of parish, this is far less likely to happen.

People will put up with all kinds of institutional inconsistencies and all manner of flawed behaviour from those distant to them, but if they are hurt by their local parish—if they feel excluded, unwanted, uncared for, uninvolved or unnoticed—this will have a far larger impact than anything perhaps the bishops might say.

Ultimately, 'thinking globally and acting locally' needs to be our approach.

Indeed, if we can transform the microcosm that is the local parish, it could be the beginning of something far greater and is likely to shape a more enduring experience of what the Church should be.

Chapter Eight
Celebrating Easter and Christmas

And when we give each other Christmas gifts in His name, let us remember that He has given us the sun and the moon and the stars, and the earth with its forests and mountains and oceans—and all that lives and moves upon them. He has given us all green things and everything that blossoms and bears fruit and all that we quarrel about and all that we have misused—and to save us from our foolishness, from all our sins, He came down to earth and gave us Himself.[1]

Sigrid Undset

There is a transcendence and a message in the image of a baby wrapped in straw, perhaps surrounded by animal refuse, and yet brought gifts of gold, frankincense and myrrh.

The ceremonies and readings of Advent and Christmas are replete with meaning, making it one of the most beautiful times in our Church's calendar.

In my childhood, my mother developed a very creative and educative ritual which gave a special symbolism to Advent. We had a little plastic nativity set, complete with Jesus (who would hide behind the trunk of the Christmas tree until after mass on Christmas Day), Mary, Joseph, donkeys, sheep, shepherds and wise men.

She would bring us children (aged ten, eight and four) together and light a purple (or a pink) candle, depending on which week of Advent we were up to.

---

1. Sigrid Undset.

We would sing the song 'Away in a Manger', and each evening, our little plastic wise men would be moved by me or my brothers a little further along the antique credenza toward our plastic Christmas tree.

It was a symbol of pilgrimage, it built our anticipation, and it was a unique and creative way of keeping Christ in Christmas.

We would excitedly retrieve Jesus from behind the Christmas tree after early-morning mass on Christmas Day and unwrap presents.

As a family, we weren't in any doubt that Christmas was a faith holiday, and that while we might not have appreciated it at the time, the greatest gift that year, and every year, was Jesus.

If there is any time of the year in which there are opportunities to display the beauty of the Church in all its splendour, Christmas would be the perfect season.

Christmas is an easy one to sell, a baby born in humble surroundings in a manger in the Middle East. Wise kings with frankincense and myrrh and gold, and swaddling clothes and a shining star for all to see. It is the uncontroversial refugee story.

One year, with this book in mind, I took notice of my surroundings as I arrived at the suburban church about ten minutes' drive from my family home.

I had been asked to lead the music and while it was going to be simple carols, we had to arrive early to set up the equipment for a large outdoor mass. As I arrived, there was a quiet, hushed feeling, and I walked in slowly.

Lines of Christmas lights had been draped from the ceiling, glistening and adding a soft dappled effect to the chairs below.

I spotted the parish priest who was casually dressed in an open-collared shirt.

This year, Christmas was falling on a Monday, so he had already said three masses in the previous twenty-four hours and would say three more that evening and one the following morning.

Not only this, but the evening masses would comprise an outdoor family mass, a traditional Vietnamese mass, and midnight mass.

At the front of the Church, a beautiful nativity had been set up—a menagerie of creatures which included, for that Aussie touch, a wombat, some beanie babies, and a koala.

'Gosh, that's the best holy family I've ever seen', remarked one older man as he wandered into the church. Indeed, hours had been spent by the parishioners to make the scene something special.

Fr Peter greeted me with a wave. 'Happy Christmas', he said, in his thickly accented English.

A former refugee who arrived in Australia by boat in the 1980s, Fr Peter is one of the most uncomplaining priests I have ever met.

He wasn't even slightly perturbed about having to say seven masses.

He was still in the thick of preparations, checking microphones, attending to the liturgical paraphernalia, moving chairs and making sure everything was working well.

He would faithfully spend an hour in the confessional each week and was almost always there to answer the presbytery door with a smile. His homilies were little stories that he told to make a salient point about the Gospel of the day, and while not always memorable, they were heartfelt.

One time, I had been having a conversation with an archbishop about useful characteristics and personality traits that helped in the priesthood.

'You know what, Beth? We need good, old reliable family sedans.'

'Oh, yes?', I asked, already having a sense of what he meant.

'Yes. They need to be flexible, go where you ask them, not make a big deal! We don't want Ferraris, you know, show ponies.'

'Ahhh ... and what about the archbishop?', I asked cheekily, knowing that this bishop was not ever going to fit the definition of a boring family sedan.

'That's different, the archbishop is different!!', he laughed, aware that all priests, like people, are made and crafted as unique individuals and that few of us will fit into a box.

Fr Peter is, however, a 'family sedan' in the best sense of the phrase, one of the GPs of the Church.

He does the hard yards, as do many. This Christmastide, he would quietly say seven masses in two different languages, and then jump in the car to drive to Western Sydney to see his ageing mother.

Some would baulk at that amount of work, but others plod along, perhaps buoyed by the sense of mission and purpose in it.

Christmas for me, until 2008, had always been the same. We would have Christmas lunch complete with prawns, cold chicken, salads and lots of wine or beer at the home of one of my cousins.

My grandfather, until that year, would always lead us in Grace. When he passed away, I became Captain Catholic and would be asked to lead the family.

In 2008, I was living in Asunción, Paraguay, and my Christmas took on a different character.

Leading into Christmas, I had been working with children between the ages of three and eighteen in an urban barrio in the northern limits of the city. Shaped by dirt roads, rubbish and animal refuse, this was a place reminiscent of the 'valley of the dry bones' (Ezk 37:1–14).

Over the summer months in Asunción, I had been spending time with around twenty young people, and I was about one and a half months into my first stint in Latin America.

My volunteer work was certainly not changing the world (as had been my original plan) but was rather a clumsy and awkward foray into learning about others in stilted and broken Spanish.

Nonetheless, my task was to give these kids something to do during the day that would literally keep them off the streets.

These young people, if not occupied, would be sent to work as recyclers, rubbish collectors, street-sellers of chewing gum and cigarettes, or singers on public buses.

Such is the reality for many of Latin America's most vulnerable young people.

Instead, we were putting together a nativity play, complete with all the characters, including a star shining in the east, played by seven-year-old Michelle, covered in crepe paper, folded tinsel, glitter and a bright smile.

As we worked together toward the final performance, there were not a few arguments. Who would play Joseph and Mary? Whose lines were not being said correctly? There were tears that someone was cast as a Shepherd when he wanted to be one of the Three Wise Men.

We practiced the song *'Feliz Navidad'* ('Happy Christmas'), and the kids took pride in getting their costumes together, collecting bits and pieces from their ramshackle homes, using masking tape and glue, and cardboard, tinsel and fabric to complete the colourful effect.

On the night of the play, a well-loved Jesuit priest came to say mass for the community. He would go on to become the Provincial of Paraguay the following year and make the choice to move his own lodgings to that impoverished barrio, instead of living in the ornate curia downtown.

There were perhaps forty of us gathered together in a chapel built for twenty, and I still remember the longing looks of those who peered in through the steel windows, wanting to get into the chapel to be part of the celebration.

After mass, we proceeded across the dirt to the school yard where we had painted a mural, and where we would perform our nativity play.

In Latin America, a nativity play is called a *'Pesebre Viviente'*, which translates as 'Living Crib'.

Dressed in a satin pink outfit adorned with lace, the Baby Jesus was laid in the manger.

Araceli, the tiniest baby in the barrio, would be *La Niñita Jesus*.

This was planned, although we were surprised at just how feminine our little baby Jesus was.

The children shone, and at the end, eagerly approached me to ask how they had gone. I had been floored by how much they had moved me, and the others who had come to watch them.

It was such a simple living crib that could not have been far from the original, and everyone present could not help but be moved as we shared sandwiches and empanadas.

Memories of that Christmas came back to me eight years later, listening to Pope Francis' homily at midnight mass at the Vatican, where he talked a little about moments where we encounter Christ in splendour, in magnificent scenes of beauty—but then, paradoxically, in the small, insignificant, boring and difficult moments.

Christmas is one of those times when perhaps we can forget the brokenness of the year with a wine or a beer, by contemplating the mystery of the baby born in the Middle East who came to save us all. But let's not be too romantic about it. For some, the opposite can be true. This is what makes it so profoundly important. Christmas can be that paradoxical time that we can feel most lonely, even when surrounded by many.

It's not just singing carols and drinking wine and eating pudding that we celebrate. It's not just the slump into a chair at the end of a long year of work that Christmas allows. It's that moment when we genuinely are invited to allow something new to be born in our hearts again, no matter what the last twelve months have brought us. It is a time, above all, to allow the light, no matter how much it has been extinguished by pain, to burn bright again.

The most important time of the liturgical year is Easter. It is what Christianity is all about, the Body of Christ given up for our sins. It's about triumph over death.

The beginning of Holy Week is marked by the Mass of Chrism, the Mass of the Oils.

In 2018, in one cathedral, the archbishop took the opportunity to reinforce just how important Easter is for us this year, and every year:

> The Church in Australia today is a bit like a Rembrandt painting. There's much light but there's also much darkness. There's the great lightness of faith-filled people who continue to give incredible witness of their love for God in their parish communities in the way they serve the poor and the marginalised. But there is also much darkness of selfishness, sin and the diabolical [referencing the findings of the Royal Commission into Institutional Responses to Child Sexual Abuse]. It is into the midst of this chiaroscuro that the Church continues to evangelise with hope and great joy.
>
> And so now the rough seas and the wounded-ness of the Australian Church today meets the Holy Week of 2018.
>
> The wounds, the death of Jesus [Good Friday], all this will give way to the Resurrected Wounds of the Risen Lord Jesus on Easter Sunday and our union in this saving encounter.
>
> It seems to be beautifully summarised in an important phrase that comes from both the New Testament and the Old that 'through His wounds we are healed'. Therefore, our faith challenge today being missionaries in this strange new context we find ourselves in Australia, is to allow the Redeemed Wounds of the Easter Jesus to heal us in our present-day wounds.[2]

Easter, and the six weeks leading up to it can be a most poignant time for churchgoers. We might start with an emptying out on Shrove Tuesday. We might make pancakes, as a symbol of using all that is good and plentiful in food. Eggs, milk and flour are poured into bowls and fried and shared.

---

2. Christopher Prowse, 'Homily: Chrism Mass 2018' at <http://cgcatholic.org.au/about/our-archbishop/homilies-teachings-pastoral-letters/homilies-2018/chrism-mass/>. Accessed 9 September 2019.

Following this is Ash Wednesday, where we receive the ashes on our foreheads.

Six weeks later we see a triumphant ride into Jerusalem and maybe we sing 'Hosanna' in the church.

This is quickly followed by a last supper with friends, and then a night of desolation and fear.

It's in recalling those scenes that we can find some hope, from a broken and anxious saviour who prayed so fervently to the point that his sweat was like drops of blood.

Our own dark nights of the soul, hours of sleeplessness, anxiety, depression might lead us to wonder where God is amid it. The Christian walk, maybe perhaps especially the Catholic version of it, does not pretend that suffering will never come. It does however look for beauty amid suffering.

There is some resonance in watching the unfolding of the events of Holy Week, and the dark night that the Australian Church is going through.

Francis Sullivan of the Church's Truth, Justice and Healing Council talks of this dark night:

> There is now a deep malaise compounded by a simmering anger within the community about the Church and child sexual abuse . . . The very fact that the church was on trial rips at the heart of what the church is meant to be. And that speaks to me of a profound loss of direction, integrity, purpose and meaning at the heart of the church. A spiritual wasteland. It is my sense that so many Catholics share that shock. People say the Church now needs to get its house back in order but I say we have to re-build the house.[3]

It might seem quaint to speak of the Royal Commission and compare it to Easter. Some might glibly say that Jesus' crucifixion happened over a short period, and that the victims of abuse have suffered often for decades.

This is more than fair.

---

3. Francis Sullivan, 'Where To from Here?', *Catalyst for Renewal Incorporated* at <http://www.tjhcouncil.org.au/media/132927/170310-SPEECH-Catalyst-for-Renewal-Hunters-Hill-Francis-Sullivan.pdf>. Accessed 9 September 2019.

Is it even possible to find resurrection or redemption amid such church-sanctioned suffering? I don't claim to know, and much needs to be done.

And yet, there is still a part of me that wants to be part of the rebuilding effort.

In 2014, I spent Holy Week in Nicaragua.

Ciudad Sandino is an urban slum next to a horrific garbage dump on the outskirts of Nicaragua's capital, Managua.

Vultures crouch above animal carcasses, dried out in the excessive heat. That rubbish dump is one of the eeriest places I have ever seen.

It was here that Holy Week took on a special synthesis as we experienced ongoing seismic events.

Small-scale earthquakes shook the country for a period of four weeks, and we lived on edge in a convent run by Compañia de Maria (Company of Mary) sisters.

On Holy Thursday, as people sat in the presence of the empty tomb, the earth shook. And as each of the nine psalms were sung by candlelight at the Easter Vigil, I observed worn faces of people who had, in some cases, moved their furniture outside to remove themselves from danger.

The whole of Nicaragua stops for the Holy Week or *Semana Santa* events. There is a donkey procession at almost every parish through the streets on Palm Sunday.

Nicaragua is one of the least visited countries in the world. Its nearest neighbour El Salvador has similar statistics. Both were places where Liberation Theology thrived, because they were home to churches, microcosms, filled with Basic Ecclesial Communities taking the reins of their parishes and enunciating their need for liberation from the social structures keeping them economically impoverished.

These crucified churches have integrated suffering in a way that we are just beginning to realise in Australia.

It's a different kind of suffering. In these countries, liberation from poverty, death squads and marginalisation were at issue.

Fr Jon Sobrino SJ, one of the great liberation theologians, narrowly escaped death when his brother Jesuits were assassinated at their residence at the University of Central America in 1989.

As he watched the footage on television in Thailand, where he was addressing a conference, he realised they were filming inside his bedroom.

He watched in horror as he noticed a book that he had been reading lying on his side table, and realised in that moment that he too would have been killed had he not been attending the conference. That book on his side table was *The Crucified God* by Jürgen Moltmann.

> When God becomes man in Jesus of Nazareth, he not only enters into the finitude of man, but in his death on the cross also enters into the situation of man's godforsakenness. In Jesus he does not die the natural death of a finite being, but the violent death of the criminal on the cross, the death of complete abandonment by God. The suffering in the passion of Jesus is abandonment, rejection by God, his Father. God does not become a religion, so that man participates in him by corresponding religious thoughts and feelings. God does not become a law, so that man participates in him through obedience to a law. God does not become an ideal, so that man achieves community with him through constant striving. He humbles himself and takes upon himself the eternal death of the godless and the godforsaken, so that all the godless and the godforsaken can experience communion with him.[4]

So, perhaps in our 'godforsakenness' as a church—that is, recognising that collectively as a church we have failed those who have been abused, and that only we can fix it—we might have the courage to walk through Holy Week and make real for those who have suffered so deeply at the hands of those abusers who actively turned their backs on Christianity, a healing and a beauty that pierces through the darkness.

---

4. Jürgen Moltmann, *The Crucified God: The Cross of Christ as the Foundation and Criticism of Christian Theology* 40th anniversary edition (Minneapolis: Fortress, 2015)

Chapter Nine
Worshipping in Spirit and Truth

The graces of a healthy prayer life will reverberate in the actions of my everyday life. I throw a stone into a quiet pond. The stone is small and the spot it touches on the surface of the water is, too. And yet its ripples expand to every corner of the lake. From that tiny spot where the rock first made contact, waves are born and are carried to the very edges. In the same way, the effects of my short period of intimate contact with God will ripple through to the very edges of my day. Many people do not understand this basic connection between their prayer lives and their everyday lives.[1]

Speak, O Lord—for your servant is listening. 1 Samuel 3:7-11

Prayer is, above all, an act of listening.

When we pray, we sit down in all kinds of places, or perhaps we go for a walk. Maybe we go on retreat or sit in the corner of a room with a mug of coffee.

Maybe we sit in community, holding hands as we recite an Our Father, or like Jesus, go off to be alone with our God. And in it, we listen.

When we pray well, we listen to the Lord and ask for that voice to 'speak into our hearts'. It is in the silence of the heart that we are most likely to hear that voice. In prayer, we are called to try to test our thoughts and attitudes in the radiance and light of God.

We ask God to rebuild the church, to inspire in us the words, phrases and actions that will tell us how to live.

---

1. Mark Thibodeaux and Mark Link, *Armchair Mystic: Easing into Contemplative Prayer* (Cincinnati, Ohio: St. Anthony Messenger Press, 2001), Chapter 15.

And what is prayer?

It is so many different things for different people.

Prayer is used to encounter the divine across faith traditions. The Buddhist, Muslim, Hindu and Jewish faiths have everything from praying the *Bhagavad Gita*— a 700-verse Hindu Scripture in Sanskrit—right through to the Jewish Saturday night celebration of *Shabbat* (The Sabbath). Muslims pray five times a day in praise of Allah, using words in Arabic from the holy Qur'an.

All these faiths have rich traditions of prayer. And within Catholicism, there are many ways of praying, stretching from *Lectio Divina*— a simple repetition of a phrase—to the Rosary, and from Imaginative Contemplation to an Examination of Conscience.

If we pray with scripture, we may just take a verse or a word, or a whole passage or a psalm. Some of us keep a journal to note down key moments or words that strike us.

A prayer for a busy mother will be a different kind of prayer to that of a monk, living in a monastery. An executive working in a senior position requiring more than fourteen hours in the office each day will likely have an entirely different approach to prayer to that of a 70-year-old grandmother who attends daily mass.

So beautiful is our Catholic tradition that it offers something for everyone, and for different personality types, too.

Indeed, throughout our lives we will adopt different styles which will make sense to us in the light of our present reality, and as we encounter new movements and experiences in our Christian walk, we will likely learn new ways to pray.

Many families have forgotten that act of saying grace at meals, and I always find it profoundly moving when I see someone eating in a restaurant and choosing to say grace in a public place. It is a public testimony to faith.

And saying grace doesn't just have to happen it mealtimes. According to GK Chesterton, it can be an 'alleluia' for all that is, in all times and places. Chesterton wrote:

> You say grace before meals.
> All right.
> But I say grace before the concert and the opera,
> And grace before the play and pantomime,
> And grace before I open a book,
> And grace before sketching, painting,

> Swimming, fencing, boxing, walking, playing, dancing
> And grace before I dip the pen in the ink.[2]

Some years ago, I interviewed a friend of mine, a mother in her thirties who now has three toddlers.

At her wedding, her brother got up to give a toast to the bride and groom, and gave some words of warning to the groom about his sister's habits:

> *My sister is addicted to retreat centres! You need to know that while you are married to her, that at any moment, she could run off to spend a week at the Abbey, praying five times a day with the Benedictines.*

The room erupted into laughter.

When it came time for our phone interview, she admitted to me that these days, as a married woman, she often found herself only able to pray a very slow, intentional 'Our Father' as she wiped soap suds from a dish at the sink. Sometimes, she would find herself asking God for the strength to wash 'just one more dish'.

Fr Richard Leonard SJ, an Australian Jesuit priest, calls himself the original extrovert; he found it difficult when he first entered the seminary to pray in silence. In his book *Why Bother Praying?* he talks about those struggles, and in one story, he writes of the experiment he was asked to do as a novice. He and one other seminarian were sent on pilgrimage in South Australia with nothing but the clothes on their back. They had to rely solely on God for their needs.

> Those ten days were the only time in my life when I've experienced hunger . . . I learned more about prayer in those ten days than in the previous twenty-five years . . . I prayed for my daily bread. I prayed for somewhere to lay my head, and I was often overwhelmed with gratitude for the smallest kindnesses.[3]

Leonard speaks of finding joy in playing the piano and singing a psalm out loud to God; he finds the discipline of daily prayer to be a

---

2. Gilbert Keith Chesterton and Aidan Mackey, *The Collected Works of GK Chesterton: [vol]. X; Collected Poetry Part 1* (San Francisco: Ignatius, 1994), 43.
3. Richard Leonard, *Why Bother Praying?* (New York: Paulist Press, 2013), 1.

struggle in a busy life. Some days he freely admits that he's lucky to get around to a 'Hail Mary', an 'Our Father' and a 'Glory Be'.

My grandmother, too, a social woman whose commitment to the most marginalised was quite unparalleled, had trouble praying. No one could do hospitality or welcome better than her, and she lived out her faith very much in action.

She had a terribly low self-image when it came to her faith.

She always felt that my grandfather was a better 'pray-er' than she was. Yet her favourite prayer, taught to her by my devout grandfather, was 'The Memorare'.

> Remember,
> O most gracious Virgin Mary,
> that never was it known that anyone who fled to thy protection,
> implored thy help or sought thy intercession,
> was left unaided.
> Inspired with this confidence,
> I fly unto thee,
> O Virgin of virgins my Mother;
> to thee do I come,
> before thee I stand,
> sinful and sorrowful;
> O Mother of thy Word Incarnate,
> despise not my petitions,
> but in thy clemency hear and answer me.
> Amen.

I had never learned 'The Memorare' until deciding to set it to music for grandma's funeral. As often happens when you repeat words over and over, they started to invade my consciousness.

I started to think of the old woman I had always known my grandma to be, who would sit there with a thimble full of scotch in a large mug of soda, smoking a cigarette and providing gentle counsel.

There were pictures of Jesus and a large portrait of John Paul II on the wall.

She had rosary beads but they didn't come out much.

Her prayer was making roast lamb with apple sauce or preparing a toasted sandwich.

It is often those most simple of prayers, like 'The Memorare', that can really express what you are trying to say, even in those moments where you can't find the words.

Of late, calligraphy and hand lettering have helped me slow down and pay attention to words, and often I practice it as I am listening in a meeting.

It's quite extraordinary how that act of focus can help me absorb more than when I am listening only.

For me, singing is how I pray best, whether it's using praise and worship music, writing my own, or spending time in the quiet of an empty church practicing music for an upcoming mass. Most of the time, it's not transcendent or mystical. Sometimes it's downright flawed.

Often, even when given a penance after the Sacrament of Reconciliation (usually some form of prayer), I will forget to do it, and hastily slam out some Hail Marys on my way to communion.

But, like exercise, it's one of those things that you notice will change you. It doesn't always do it instantly. Sometimes it's an arid, hard slog that seems to produce no results. Sometimes, it's like running up hill on a treadmill. Other times, it's like drinking from a cool fountain in a hot desert.

We exercise because we know it's good for us, but sometimes we don't see the results for months or even years.

There is something of an analogy for prayer which is provided by our digital age, an era where we are sometimes too connected. We are less and less able to sit in the silence, with the ding of Snapchat or the click of the keys as we hammer out a comment on Instagram.

Yet, perhaps now more than ever, there is a need for us to be constantly seeking out that 'wi-fi hotspot' of God's grace, God's voice in prayer.

That said, as seasoned pray-ers and mystics know, the signal strength of God's voice does not pop up on the corner of the screen letting us know how long our download is likely to take.

There are no bars indicating how good our connection might be. The signal strength is sometimes weak, and at times the reception is bad.

Sometimes there is too much traffic on the network.

And perhaps sometimes, the effects of perseverance in the search for God's spirit are only discernible later, in retrospect.

For me, the most powerful and enduring form of prayer has been music. It is how I worship; it is how I make sense of the ins and outs, the peaks and troughs of life. Music was also important for many people surveyed, and bad music in a parish can have a huge impact on people's experience of prayer.

'Is it too much to ask that the person leading worship can actually sing?', opined the Religious Education Coordinator at my school one week, having attended mass at a parish and finding the music to be less than mediocre.

It was St Augustine who said: 'When we sing, we pray twice.' Indeed, there's something that happens when words are put to song, when notes and words are arranged together in such a way that they raise our hearts and minds in worship.

> Choir members, like all liturgical ministers should exercise their ministry with evident faith and should participate in the entire liturgical celebration, recognising that they are servants of the liturgy and members of the gathered assembly.[4]

Stepping into the church of my youth early last year, accompanying my mother, I was flooded with memories.

A large projection screen rolled down mechanically, and the guitarists started tuning up.

A volunteer pulled out the computer to operate the PowerPoint slides. I couldn't help remembering the days where we did it all on overhead projectors. On the weeks where my youth choir and I would write our own hymns, back in the 1990s, the words would be neatly written onto transparent sheets with permanent markers and we'd run them by Father for the mandatory heresy check.

My mother's choir is one of the post-Vatican II folk variety. We call them the 'Saturday Night Seekers' in jest, and I think they quite enjoy the comparison.

It is such a beautiful little community of singers that no-one, not even the parish priest has the heart to suggest a change in repertoire. The parishioners seem to like it too. It's one of the uniting and ordinary things about suburban Catholicism.

This parish isn't packed. Likely it will be amalgamated in a few short years when there are no longer enough priests to service all the area's parishes. However, it's a tight-knit little community of mostly middle-class parishioners.

---

4. United States Conference of Catholic Bishops and Catholic Church, *Sing To the Lord: Music in Divine Worship* (Washington, DC: United States Conference of Catholic Bishops, 2007), 32.

My mother has been learning the guitar, and has been playing 'third guitar', one chord a line, for the past few months.

I nervously listen, wondering if the parishioners are silently wishing she would go back to her colourful array of percussion instruments, but she's doing okay, and the joy it gives her is worth it.

Music has kept me in the Church, and yet, it has been such a source of suffering for me at times that I feel it is worth mentioning in a book about the Church.

The Catholic Church, in all its universality, is home to a vast array of musical traditions. There have been entire books dedicated to the good, the bad and the ugly of it. Indeed, there was one book titled *Why Catholics Can't Sing: The Culture of Catholicism and the Triumph of Bad Taste* by Thomas Day.[5]

The official teaching of the Church on music says the following:

> Liturgical worship is given a more noble form when it is celebrated in song, with the ministers of each degree fulfilling their ministry and the people participating in it. Indeed, through this form, prayer is expressed in a more attractive way, the mystery of the liturgy, with its hierarchical and community nature, is more openly shown, the unity of hearts is more profoundly achieved by the union of voices, minds are more easily raised to heavenly things by the beauty of the sacred rites, and the whole celebration more clearly prefigures that heavenly liturgy which is enacted in the holy city of Jerusalem.[6]

But, for all this beautiful writing on the purpose of Catholic music, there is also the reality.

Those of us who attend Catholic parishes frequently have probably experienced the plethora of options ranging from the eighty-five-year-old playing the organ with a traditional repertoire lifted from *The Catholic Worship Book* to the majestic cathedral choir complete with four-part harmony and the folky choirs complete with guitars, cymbals, triangles and tambourines.

---

5. Thomas Day, *Why Catholics Can't Sing: The Culture of Catholicism and the Triumph of Bad Taste*. (New York: Crossroad, 1990).
6. Vatican.va, *Musicam Sacram: Instruction on Music in the Liturgy*, 5 March 1967 at http://www.vatican.va/archive/hist_councils/ii_vatican_council/documents/vat-ii_instr_19670305_musicam-sacram_en.html. Accessed 9 September 2019.

Then there are the young adult groups who might be more likely to include some praise and worship music drawn from Hillsong or Bethel Music.

Some of the younger generations, perhaps those of us raised among World Youth Days, might be more liturgically conservative than our parents' generation, so we might mix it up a bit by playing from the 'Green Book', but then maybe using something a little more charismatic, or alternatively, pious.

A popular trend recently has been the music of artists like Matt Maher, Fr Rob Galea and Audrey Assad who blend traditional Catholic beliefs with a modern style of music.

Having reflected deeply on these questions and humbly aware that I haven't always gotten the song choices right, the question was recently posed to me: 'What happens when, regardless of the style of music, it is just not played well?'

Many of us might have experienced that moment in parishes where loud, badly played, out-of-tune music starts up after communion, just as we settle down to pray, and rather than helping, it can hinder the moment.

I was discussing this with a parish priest who had just become the head pastor at a large, amalgamated parish. He was having difficulty with the fact that there were eleven different music groups in the parish, which offers four masses on a Sunday. He shared his view that it's crucially important to get the balance of musical styles right. It can make the difference for people between which parish they attend and which they avoid.

Catholic music is an interesting genre because sometimes a song might work in a particular context, and other times not so much.

World Youth Day, that event that brings together young Catholics from across the world is a melting pot or microcosm in which we can analyse how liturgical music is used.

World Youth Days (WYD) are full of stirring anthems. Even the least popular of the WYD songs can get a group going, dancing around despite sleep deprivation and language barriers. Some better-known songs can induce flash mobs of people waving their arms and untunefully belting out lyrics in the middle of the street during the weeks leading up to the event.

One of the strengths of this type of music is that it is usually, among other things, well-rehearsed and prayerfully written. It achieves a level of excellence because much time, reflection and liturgical knowledge is put into it. This type of preparation is not always seen elsewhere.

If we in Catholic parishes were better at seeing all liturgies, all masses, as equally important, as celebrating a sacred mystery, perhaps we would have the double effect of seeing more people in our churches on a Sunday and a more beautiful celebration.

But then again? Why is it important?

I think of the impact that the music ministry of the churches has had on my own faith formation. It was through music that I came to know the scriptures, to understand something of the story of faith and know something of the nature of God. Songs which might ordinarily make us cringe with their simplicity, their seemingly banal lyrics, and their unusual translations, unite us.

If the purpose of liturgical music is to lead others into prayer, what happens when it does the opposite?

What happens when the music ministry no longer draws people and communities together, but instead provides an opportunity for individuals to shine or to frustrate and hinder a congregation? Personally, I've struggled with this over many years. We need to ask ourselves about our Christ-like values of inclusion, but also, attend to the beauty of the liturgy. And, inclusion must win out.

The most important thing is balancing the prayer life of the parish, the building up of the community with appropriate liturgical worship, with the needs of people who seek to be included in the music ministry, even if, as they say, they don't always sing from the same song sheet.

In their book *Sing! How Worship Transforms Your Life, Family, and Church*, songwriters Keith and Kristin Getty write that God wants us all to sing—if we can speak, we can sing: 'He's far less concerned with your tunefulness than your integrity. Christian singing begins with the heart, not the lips (Eph 5:19).'[7]

---

7. Keith Getty and Kristyn Getty, *Sing! How Worship Transforms Your Life, Family, and Church* (Nashville: B&H Publishing, 2017), 2.

Chapter Ten
Let Justice Roll Down

I felt that the Church was the Church of the poor . . . but at the same time, I felt that it did not set its face against a social order which made so much charity in the present sense of the word necessary. I felt that charity was a word to choke over. Who wanted charity? And it was not just human pride but a strong sense of man's dignity and worth, and what was due to him in justice, that made me resent, rather than feel proud of so mighty a sum total of Catholic institutions.[1]

Catholic Social Teaching is often referred to as the best-kept secret of the Church.

Indeed, anyone who is aware of the breadth of beautiful, consistent and life-affirming teaching across social justice issues would be in no doubt of the Church's preferential option for the poor, even if it is lived out imperfectly, including at the highest levels.

The Bible too is unequivocal about the distribution of resources in the world. It is clear in both the Old and New Testaments that service to the poor is not an optional extra for people of faith.

It is clear too that there is currently no political party in the world that has come close to espousing these values in a manner that is consistent with, or even mildly reminiscent of, the Gospel, and that includes those parties with Christian names, or that have card-carrying Christians as their leaders.

We don't always express the richness of Catholic Social Teaching well as an institutional Church, and so perhaps Catholics can be forgiven for a lack of formation in these areas.

---

1. Day, *The Long Loneliness*, 150.

Movements such as Caritas, Catholic Mission, St Vincent de Paul, and local charities and justice groups sometimes find little more than lip service from the hierarchy to support their work.

In addition to this, there is still a significant culture of opulence, perhaps especially among Church leaders, and some of the most admirable church leaders I've met seem to have a blind spot in this area of social justice.

Shane Claiborne, author of *The Irresistible Revolution*, wrote of this tension:

> I asked participants who claimed to be 'strong followers of Jesus' whether Jesus spent time with the poor. Nearly 80 percent said yes. Later in the survey, I sneaked in another question, I asked this same group of strong followers whether they spent time with the poor, and less than 2 percent said they did. I learned a powerful lesson: We can admire and worship Jesus without doing what he did. We can applaud what he preached and stood for without caring about the same things. We can adore his cross without taking up ours. I had come to see that the great tragedy of the church is not that rich Christians do not care about the poor but that rich Christians do not know the poor.[2]

One of my survey respondents stressed the importance of charitable work, and while scandalised in many ways, said that much of the justice tradition is why she stayed:

> Sometimes I wonder why I stay. The Royal Commission [into Institutional Responses to Sexual Abuse] certainly caused me to question. But there is more good in the Church than those who betrayed the trust placed in them. I also love that the church reaches out to the poor and marginalised through works of charity and hospitals and so many other ways, this I think really keeps me faithful to the church.

In 2014, I met an inspiring young woman called Kerry Weber who is the managing editor at *America Magazine*, a Jesuit journal based in New York.

---

2. Shane Claiborne, *The Irresistible Revolution: Living as an Ordinary Radical* (Grand Rapids, Michigan: Zondervan, 2006), 70.

That year, she won the Christopher Award for the best piece of Catholic writing with her book *Mercy in the City: How to Feed the Hungry, Give Drink To the Thirsty, Visit the Imprisoned, and Keep Your Day Job*.[3] The Christopher Awards are for media, in various categories, that 'affirm the highest values of the human spirit'. Weber was one of the winners in the Adult Book category. The book is a marvel.

Basically, when in her late twenties and during the season of Lent, this young woman decided to embark upon a mission to perform all Corporal Works of Mercy over the forty-day Lenten period, and to document her progress.

In *Mercy in the City*, Weber quotes Basil the Great, who offers a challenge to all of us about how we might better live:

> The bread which you do not use is the bread of the hungry; the garment hanging in your wardrobe is the garment of him who is naked; the shoes that you do not wear are the shoes of the one who is barefoot; the money that you keep locked away is the money of the poor; the acts of charity that you do not perform are so many injustices that you commit.[4] (St Basil the Great, in Weber, 2014.)

In saying that, not all of us are called to be Dorothy Day or Mother Teresa, or even to imitate Kerry Weber who takes on special tasks during Lent. Rather, we are asked to think about where we can stretch ourselves to live more sacrificially, more simply, so that others might simply live.

So many of us comfortably go about our Christianity without questioning unjust social structures.

Australian Catholicism has known some persecution, but much of it is self-inflicted. We cannot say that we are a 'persecuted people'.

I'm sure that most of you reading this book have most of the essential things you need, and can access, simply by being born in a developed country, resources to better your situation.

Indeed, this makes sense within our practice of faith too. While we might think by accumulate all manner of indulgences through

---

3. Kerry Weber, *Mercy in the City: How To Feed the Hungry, Give Drink To the Thirsty, Visit the Imprisoned, and Keep Your Day Job* (Chicago: Loyola Press, 2014).
4. Weber, *Mercy in the City*

prayer and mass attendance that this is the be all and end all our faith, often, in fact, this still leads to emptiness. Unless we pour ourselves out in giving to others, we find that there is a distinct lack of meaning in our lives.

In 2004 and again in 2005–6, I found myself at a home for alcoholic men in the Melbourne suburb of Fitzroy. The Way was at least nominally Catholic, and so were most of its volunteers. One of the main founders of The Way went on to become a Jesuit priest.

The men who lived there were generally middle-aged, and most had suffered from alcoholism for a large portion of their lives. All had at least some experience of homelessness.

Each week, there would be a community mass, where all would be invited to participate in the liturgy, whether they identified as Catholic or not. They would choose the songs they would sing from a small hymnal, and inevitably there would come a request for Loreto Sr Deirdre Brown's 'Come as You Are'.

They requested this hymn because it gave them a sense of comfort that even they, broken as they felt themselves to be, were deserving of the love of God.

What could be more beautiful than breaking bread together in this way, than Jesus sharing his life with men who might call themselves broken, but who show up, 'as they are'?

It is a welcome from a God who proclaims that all are welcome, especially those who are at the margins.

And yet, we don't always do this. There is plenty of historical evidence that we in the Church have had the teaching of Jesus regarding the poor clearly spelled out for us; yet we've ignored it.

Caritas Internationalis often uses the slain Archbishop of San Salvador, Óscar Romero, as an exemplar of justice and a preferential option for the poor.

Archbishop Romero, who was canonised in 2018, was killed in 1980. During his lifetime, he was a voice crying in the wilderness. He was marginalised and alone amongst his brother bishops, and was eventually assassinated while saying mass, because of his weekly cries, via long homilies, urging an end to the repression of the suffering majority of Salvadorans.

In that Central American country, church workers and campesinos, politicians and peasants were systematically killed over a period of more than twenty years. Most of them were poor or were those who spoke out in service and defence of the poor.

> When I give to the poor they call me a saint. But when I ask why it is that they have no food to eat, they call me a communist.[5]

This quote is perhaps the most famous from the Brazilian Catholic Bishop of Olinda and Recife, Dom Hélder Câmara (1909–99), who was, some say, a liberation theologian before the term was coined later in the twentieth century.

American journalist, Penny Lernoux, herself a Catholic, saw the disconnect between the actions of people in the Church, and the teachings of Christ, and made it her business to speak out.

> At stake are two different visions of faith, the Church of Caesar, powerful and rich; and the Church of Christ—loving, poor and spiritually rich.[6]

Such prophets are still few and far between.

I truly believe that only when we have adequately asked ourselves if we are genuinely living out Christ's call—the preferential option for the most marginalised in society—will we truly understand the meaning of what it is to live faith in action.

Today, in my local Catholic church, I still see the purchase of marble floors and expensive sound systems in preference to additional service provision for the vulnerable people of my city.

I've seen Church properties refurbished to service an ever-decreasing number of priests, while at the same time people with mental illness cry out for services.

A relatively newly ordained priest of my home diocese began his homily one day with sentiments of righteous anger.

On the day he delivered his homily, there was a packed Church and it's safe to say he ruffled some feathers. No feathers were ruffled more than those of the diminutive nuns in the blue and white saris, one of whom took him to task for some words he had spoken on contraception.

---

5. Dom Helder Câmara, and Francis McDonagh, *Dom Helder Camara* (Maryknoll, NY: Orbis Books, 2009), 13.
6. Penny Lernoux, *People of God: The Struggle for World Catholicism* (New York: Viking, 1989), 1.

She marched up into the sanctuary, took hold of the microphone, and made her piece known.

Within one five-minute homily, this priest had managed to touch on just about every hot button issue imaginable.

But what has stayed with me from that day were not his remarks about contraception or any number of other things that I now can't remember, but the quote, repeated above, from Hélder Câmara.

This local Australian priest was not only doing the work of serving the poor, he was going deeper into questions of why. He was not satisfied with a handout, he wanted to break the bonds that keep people poor.

As mentioned previously, Catholic Social Teaching has in some ways been the church's best kept secret, but it is not without its critics. More than once recently, I've seen social media debates about what some consider to be the 'liberal agenda of Catholic schools', criticising them for focusing more on 'social justice initiatives' than on 'meeting the person of Jesus Christ'.

But, if Catholic schools do not start with justice, what God are we following? St James' epistle is quite clear in its call to faith and works:

> What good is it, my brothers and sisters, if you say you have faith but do not have works? Can faith save you? If a brother or sister is naked and lacks daily food, and one of you says to them, 'Go in peace; keep warm and eat your fill', and yet you do not supply their bodily needs, what is the good of that? So, faith by itself, if it has no works, is dead. (Jas 2:14–26)

The diminutive nun who founded the Missionaries of Charity, Mother Teresa, was frequently quoted as saying that when she treated the poorest of the poor in the slums of Kolkata or when she held a child dying of starvation in Beirut, she would encourage her sisters and lay workers to see the image of Christ in the distressing disguise of the poor. Even for one with such a call, she shared with her biographer Malcolm Muggeridge that it took her weeks to become accustomed to the stench of the poor people to whom she ministered.

In 2013, Pope Francis called on the world's priests to stay close to the marginalised and to be 'shepherds living with the smell of the sheep'.

Those priests 'who do not go out of themselves' by being mediators between God and men can 'gradually become intermediaries, managers', he said on 28 March during the Chrism Mass in St Peter's Basilica.[7]

One of the most famous stories of St Francis of Assisi, from whom Pope Francis takes his name, is of sighting a leper, and initially being repulsed. Reflecting on his reaction, Francis overcame it, and responded by taking the toe of the leper into his mouth.

Ron Rolheiser OMI writes that 'kissing the leper' will be where our most fundamental home in Christ will be found:

> 'Whatsoever you do to the least of my people, that you do unto to me,' Christ assures us. In the poor, God is ever-present in our world, waiting to be met. In the powerless, one can find the power of God; in the voiceless, one can hear the voice of God; in the economically poor, one can find God's treasures; in the weak, one can find God's strength; and in the unattractive, one can find God's beauty.
>
> The glory of God might indeed be humanity fully alive, but the privileged presence of God lies especially in and with the poor.
>
> Thus, like Francis, we need to get off our horses and kiss the leper. If we do, something will snap, we will see our pampered lives for what they are, and God and love will break into our lives in such a way that we will never be the same again.[8]

Psalm 139:14 reminds us that each one of us, including the leper, is created in the image and likeness of God. We are each clothed in dignity.

As a way of emphasising the dignity of all persons, Joseph Cardinal Bernardin used the term 'Consistent Ethic of Life' calling it 'The Seamless Garment'—echoing the seamlessness of Jesus' burial shroud.[9]

---

7. Pope Francis, *Chrism Mass: Homily, Saint Peter's Basilica (Holy Thursday, 28 March 2013)* at <http://w2.vatican.va/content/francesco/en/homilies/2013/documents/papa-francesco_20130328_messa-crismale.html>. Accessed 10 September 2019.
8. Ron Rolheiser, 'Kissing the Leper', *Ron Rolheiser, OMI* at http://ronrolheiser.com/kissing-the-leper/#.XQHsz4gzbIV. Accessed 9 September 2019.
9. Joseph Bernardin and Thomas Nairn, *The Seamless Garment: Writings on the Consistent Ethic of Life* (Maryknoll, NY: Orbis Books, 2008).

For generations, political parties have sold themselves on one or other platform.

The use different issues of the day to stake their positions and to align themselves with the ideologies they espouse.

The words 'seamless garment' denote a technique in where the seams or lines of a fabric are not visible, they flow together in unity, each part of the fabric equally important.

This also refers to Christ's burial cloth, representing of course that Christ's body, the Church, is wrapped in a fabric, clothed in a dignity, and that very fabric is made up of many parts that work together in unity.

In 1982, Joseph Cardinal Bernardin's idea was that all issues involving human life should be treated with the utmost importance.

This perhaps doesn't sound all that original to those involved in church or politics, but it is based around the idea that all human life is sacred.

It's not rocket science. It's been said before. So why bring it up here?

In 2010, while attending a meeting with some active church personnel, I was struck by the breadth of the conversation.

It made me wonder, as I often had in the past, what a Catholic might automatically think of when the words 'life issues' are used?

In *America Magazine* in 2019, Michael O'Loughlin addressed to this idea when reporting on the United States Conference of Catholic Bishops' election of a Chairman for the Bishops' Pro Life Committee Issues. So heated is the debate in the United States Church that many of the bishops abstained from the vote, and an archbishop was chosen over a cardinal.

When we in the Australian Church think of life issues, I would venture to say that issues such as abortion, euthanasia, stem-cell research, and surrogacy are high up on the list in people's minds.

Further along the continuum comes discussion of contraception, marriage and family, and what all of this means in our society.

The Life Council in the Catholic Church, however, has a far broader reach than this, and I think an excellent model for how we might work together to uphold that most important of Catholic Social Teachings, human dignity.

This meeting of that Life Council was characterised by heartfelt conversation and empathy for people who had suffered sexual abuse, refugees and asylum seekers, people experiencing homelessness, indigenous people, women who had suffered the grief of abortion, and people living with disabilities.

Just a week prior to this meeting, however, I had witnessed a heated debate on social media when a young friend of mine had shared a photo of himself shaking the hand of a politician known for controversial stands on life issues.

Other friends had jumped on him, accusing him of 'shaking hands with the devil, and condoning his policies on abortion'.

Much vitriol ensued, and it prompted me to write about this issue, recognising that these friends of mine—on both sides of the debate—were profoundly good people, with highly formed Catholic consciences.

All of them had engaged in some theological study beyond what was provided in their respective Catholic schools, and so none could have been called ignorant.

How they had arrived at such polar opposite positions seemed a mystery. However, it was less of a mystery when I considered that both sides were defending the sanctity of human life in some respect. It's just that they saw different faces of the issue.

My friend who shared the photo was shaking hands with a politician he saw as a defender of refugees and the environment, a politician who would perhaps take a utilitarian approach to ethical questions.

My other friend was from a family to the right of the political divide, who saw the early stages of human life as key and would perhaps have taken a more deontological approach to ethics.

It made me think about human life, in all its forms, and how one of the great strengths of the Catholic Church is its focus on the sacred value of each human being.

It also made me think of politics, and how we frame such issues. It made me think of the traditional and somewhat incorrect economic terms placed on people.

Lefties, liberals, right-wingers, bleeding hearts, conservatives are just a few of the expressions we all use at times to create distinction. None of them are helpful.

Indeed, a challenge I would put to all, myself included, is to start considering the importance we place on life issues in their entirety.

I would challenge those who champion one cause and not another to consider how their causes might relate to each other by the very virtue of our creation in the image of God.

Put simply, refugee advocates, pro-life advocates and all people of good will would have a far more effective voice if they worked together and affirmed one another. One of the biggest challenges to unity in our Church are those who become caught up in single-issue politics.

The media love to pitch bishops and politicians against each other, particularly when they all proclaim some united faith, in order to generate factions or create controversy and stir up a fight.

One of the beautiful things I have seen recently among many of my work colleagues are people who characterise Bernardin's 'Consistent Ethic of Life'. And the reason for this may just be that they are seeking to imitate Christ.

The Church in Australia and around the world needs to get better at this uniting together on all of the important issues of life.

Most of us struggle with this, but it is the very essence of the Christian walk. And we must ask the question constantly: How might we bring about justice and a civilisation of love which affirms each stage of life in all its messiness and beauty?

Chapter Eleven
Rebuilding, Renewal, Reform

Let nothing disturb you,
Let nothing frighten you,
All things are passing away:
God never changes.
Patience obtains all things
Whoever has God lacks nothing;
God alone suffices.[1]

St Teresa of Avila

It takes some courage to be Catholic today, to profess, to practice, to live out, to witness and to believe.

In the final months of completing this text, I visited a number of different parishes.

I had recently moved to a new house, and I started to sample some of the local parishes in my area to see which one might help me to grow in faith.

Suffice to say it was difficult as I experienced woeful liturgies, one after another.

One priest expressed to me one of his own struggles about how liturgy is celebrated:

> We've turned a domestic family meal into an often cultic ritual sacrifice. I think there's a real hunger for kitchen-table Catholicism, but I don't mean that in the sense of a folksy, Kum-bah-yah-my-Lord thing, what I mean is we need that intimacy, mutuality. But what does that look like? It's very respectful

---

1. Teresa of Avila.

> of the beauty of the liturgy, but there's a domestic side. I'm not talking about dumbing it down at all, but when a family meal becomes exclusive . . . if you open a restaurant or have a wedding . . . and say come along to the feast, to the wedding reception, but if you're married or divorced you have to sit over there, etc., you'd be laughed out of town. The mass should be the most welcoming, humble, open door thing and I just call it institutional blasphemy when it's not.

It was a sombre feeling in the church in late December 2017. Empty pews greeted us, and our shoes on the marble floors seemed noisy and hollow. There was just one man and his two kids praying in an otherwise deserted building.

Christmas was only days away, and the Royal Commission into Institutional Responses to Child Sexual Abuse had handed down its final report a week earlier.

It was sobering reading for the investigated institutions, but the Catholic Church, on a brief skim through the report, was the clear forerunner in its failure.

This was not unfair. The Catholic Church was overwhelmingly represented among the institutions operating during the period of the commission's terms of reference.

To be clear, here are the figures from the final report:

> Catholic Church authorities provided information about claims of child sexual abuse they received between 1 January 1980 and 28 February 2015 (the Catholic Church claims data). Of the 201 Catholic Church authorities surveyed, 92 authorities (46 per cent) reported having received one or more claims of child sexual abuse. Overall, 4,444 claimants alleged incidents of child sexual abuse in 4,756 reported claims to Catholic Church authorities.[2]

Among the Royal Commission's key recommendations was the abolition of the seal of the confessional, to enable priests to report abuse disclosed to them during the Sacrament of Reconciliation. The recommendation wasn't one the Commission appreciated or understood.

---

2. Australia. Royal Commission into Institutional Responses to Child Sexual Abuse, 'Religious Institutions', *Royal Commission into Institutional Responses to Child Sexual Abuse: Religious Institutions* at <https://www.childabuseroyalcommission.gov.au/religious-institutions>. Accessed 9 September 2019.

On the day of my church visit, I had arrived about fifteen minutes early for the Second Rite of Reconciliation with my mother. (My mother prefers the quick nature of this form of the rite.) The toilets were locked, only the side door of the cathedral was open.

'Maybe I got the night wrong', I thought to myself and looked quizzically at my mother.

I had made sure to check which location for the second rite would be most convenient for us and we had jointly decided on the cathedral, perhaps cheekily, for the wide variety of priests we might choose from.

A quick scan of my phone showed that it was indeed happening, and at just a few minutes to the hour, the priests started to drift in, their vestments and purple stoles draped over their arms. We greeted those we knew as they walked in and watched as other people entered the cathedral.

By the time the service started at 7:30pm, the cathedral was not even five per cent full. Many of those I knew were from out of area but preferred the cathedral to their own parishes for one reason or another.

Maybe ten people from the parish itself had assembled. The numbers were more than sobering; they were a symptom of people's feelings about their Church. In previous years, the numbers had already been dwindling, but on this night, there were just a very few faithful, clinging on, perhaps by their fingernails.

The service began with a mournful Advent song, 'O Come, O Come, Emmanuel'.

To me it has a sad tone, nothing about it speaks of joy and expectation, and it set the tone for the evening.

We were then led in an examination of conscience by a distracted, serious priest.

I'm still not sure why he decided to mention that penitents should be aware of the nature of a second rite, but it made an already chilly reception seem even colder:

> *This is not a counselling session. You approach the priest, you don't need to make the sign of the cross or an act of contrition. You tell the priest your sins, and then you return to your seat.*

I raised my eyebrows, a little shocked at the tone, and frustrated by it.

Why would a priest further discourage people from attending the sacraments?

Why not encourage the faithful? This was such an opportunity to let the Church be a balm for hungry souls, people who had made time at the busiest season of the year to make an act of faith, however imperfect.

Even if each person in the cathedral had ten minutes with one of the six priests, everyone would have been out of there in less than an hour. As it was, the whole thing was over in twenty minutes.

One priest found himself in a confessional box that didn't have a single person come to it. He gave up after fifteen minutes.

The whole affair was sad, and symptomatic of a wider malaise, maybe even a distrust of the Church.

As I debriefed it with my mother, she mentioned that there was probably a deep sense of mistrust, and that the confessional box had probably put people off.

And yet, it continues to become apparent to me, over the many times I attend an imperfect, broken, reactionary or stale liturgy, that God is still amongst it.

God is also present with those who didn't attend church that night, preferring Christmas shopping or family dinner or any number of other perfectly legitimate things. So why choose church?

Timothy Radcliffe OP, the former Master General of the Dominicans wrote in his book *Why Go To Church?*:

> Going to mass does not mean that we shall be filled with warm feelings for other members of the congregation. Probably not! But it does imply a gradual transformation of who I am—'I and no longer I'—discovering God and myself in the stranger, and God in the core of my being... The slow working of grace will free me to be sent at the end. Why go to Church? To be sent from it.[3]

Perhaps the most interesting (albeit the briefest by a long shot) interview I did with someone who no longer attends church was that done over lunch at a pub in Albury with my dad.

---

3. Timothy Radcliffe, *Why Go to Church?: The Drama of the Eucharist* (London: Continuum, 2009).

Dad stopped attending mass regularly in about 2000. There was no one reason for it and he never really spoke about his decision. I was surprised that as I read some of the answers from the survey to my parents that dad wanted to do it himself.

When he answered my questions, the one that most interested me was why he doesn't go to church and what he finds beautiful.

He doesn't go because 'it has no relevance to his life', and 'because of the witness (or lack thereof) of other Christians'.

What would make him return? 'The bells and the smells—the sense of tradition.'

He went back to his beer, but it was interesting then to attend the funeral the following day. It was a secular ceremony in a funeral home. There were some heartfelt tributes, a PowerPoint presentation, a couple of non-religious songs from the 1970s, and some plastic flowers laid on a coffin.

While it was nice in its own way, it lacked the beauty of a long-standing tradition, and fair enough, this family member had not grown up within a Catholic tradition.

His daughter closed her tribute with some verses from the Gospel of John.

It was the only religious element in the entire service.

Such profound words were spoken by her, that I felt a sadness, a sadness that he had never had the opportunity to grow up in a home that had truly embraced the flawed beauty of Christianity.

So often we attend to our religious observance with a broken heart. We cling on by our fingernails. We despair. Sometimes, we rise from the ashes; other times, we stay in the sorrow.

Audrey Assad writes of this temptation to despair in much of her music. As a Christian songwriter in the Catholic tradition, she draws from a wellspring of personal faith and from the fundamentalist tradition that she grew up in.

Yet even she admits to serious doubts. Upon recording her hymns album *Inheritance*, released at the beginning of 2015, she admitted that she was almost unable to record it, because she was no longer sure if she believed any of it.

She was so distressed at the situation of the Church in the world and of her own personal faith, that she had nothing left.

In a recent concert, Assad spoke about the solace she found in Mother Teresa's story, recounted in *Come Be My Light*, which shows that even that great saint had experienced some twenty or thirty years of complete spiritual darkness.

Brian Kolodiejchuk collected the writings of 'The Saint of Calcutta' into the collection *Come Be My Light* more than a decade after her death, and from Mother Teresa's letters and journal entries, prayers and notes, Kolodiejchuk summed up what she experienced thus:

> To commit herself to becoming 'an apostle of Joy' when humanly speaking she might have felt at the brink of despair, was heroic indeed. She could do so because her joy was rooted in the certitude of the ultimate goodness of God's loving plan for her. And though her faith in this truth did not touch her soul with consolation, she ventured to meet the challenges of life with a smile. Her one lever was her blind trust in God.[4]

Assad's compositions carry some of this same pain, though expressed through the perspective of an artist and poet.

As part of *Inheritance*, Assad only included a couple of original compositions, and one of those resonates with those of us who experience doubt. Her song, 'Even Unto Death' is a stunning reflection on the cruel martyrdom of twelve Egyptian Coptic Christians killed by ISIS in 2014.[5]

The song, best listened to with the context in mind, illustrates beautifully just how much we need to seek beauty from ashes, even as we walk through our own Gethsemane.

> When we lay the soil of our hard lives open to the rain of grace and let joy penetrate our cracked and dry places, let joy soak into our broken skin and deep crevices, life grows. How can this not be the best thing for the world? For us?[6]

About 30,000 words into this project, I was beginning to doubt this book had legs. When I went to Reconciliation with an eighty-three-year-old priest who had been sixty years in this diocese, I was feeling more and more frustrated with the wider Church.

---

4. Mother Teresa and Brian Kolodiejchuk, *Come Be My Light: The Private Writings of the 'Saint of Calcutta'*. (New York: Doubleday, 2007), 171.
5. Audrey Assad, 'Even unto Death', in *Inheritance* [CD] (n.p.: Fortunate Fall Records, 2016).
6. Ann Voskamp, *One Thousand Gifts: A Dare To Live Fully Right Where You Are* (Grand Rapids, Mich: Zondervan, 2012), 58.

Within ten minutes of conversation, he had managed to restore some hope.

At the time, I had been reading a bit of the Bible every night. Something from the Old Testament, something from the New Testament, and a Psalm.

As this elderly priest spoke to me about Christ's mercy, he mentioned Psalm 102.

Just the evening before I had landed upon Psalm 101, meaning that night's Psalm would be 102.

Coincidence or God-incidence?

We began to talk about the temptation to despair and loneliness in the Church, the future, the scandals. He spoke to me about humanity, and the mystical body of Christ. His words washed over me, and I thought, 'exactly'. It is moments like this that remind me of why I stay. It is my home, my community, my communion. It is a broken home in many ways. It can be painful to stay, but I would prefer to try to repair it than walk away.

It seemed that most of those who responded to my survey felt the same, with all kinds of stories to share about why they despair and why they stay. For many of them, including Francis Sullivan, the ongoing theme was the phrase, 'where else would I go?'

One particularly vivid response went as follows:

> For its failings, it is Christ's body in the world. Christ loves the Church ('Christ loved the church and gave himself up for her', Eph 5:25), knowing full well her brokenness. He loved the Church when one of its leaders had betrayed him, its main leader had denied he knew him, and the others had run away.
>
> I can't be pickier than Jesus was, more judgemental and condemnatory of the Church than he was. If I want to be united to Jesus, I need to be united to his body. That's the big picture. Day to day—it is the Church that gives me the Eucharist, that ministers Jesus' forgiveness to me. It's the Church, which for all its difficulty living as Christ wants us to live, teaches us how he wants us to live. The Church gives me living witnesses— and many dead ones—to heroism, to heroic virtue, to selfless service—people I have known personally, whom I've read about in our time and in the past, who inspire me with a vision of what it is possible for humans to be, by the grace of Christ.

> And doctrines—wonderful, mysterious doctrines which carefully avoid simplistic answers on one side or the other and give us access to the mystery of who God is, who Christ is, who the Church is, who we are as human beings.
>
> And in our time, I see the Church as virtually alone as an institution that can stand up to forces of evil, of destructiveness, of false thinking, of confusion about sexuality, of senseless killing of the unborn, of abuse of government power and so much else.

And so, for me, the Church is not only true, but it is a place where I can be who I am, and still be a daughter of God. I can sin, and through the Sacrament of Reconciliation, experience in a tangible way the mercy of God. And, as I kept speaking to others about this project, I realised how important communion is, and I started thinking of all my different church communities.

We find in our various ways a common purpose, togetherness, sharing. Put another way, community. According to Dorothy Day, in her spiritual classic *The Long Loneliness*, community is the antidote to loneliness.

And so, in the Catholic tradition, there is no answer but community. Even the most introverted among us become more fully ourselves in relationship with others.

It is this witness, and this type of action, that will save the Church, even in countries like Australia. A Church of the poor, a Church that goes to the edges and beyond, to the peripheries.

In planning for 2020's Plenary Council, we must go to the peripheries. We need to respond to this opportunity of renewal with hearts open, but as Joan Chittister argues, we need to question along the way, too:

> We suckle ourselves on clear or comfortable answers because we fear to ask the questions that make the real difference to the quality and content of our souls. The spiritual life begins when we discover that we can only become spiritual adults when we go beyond the answers, beyond the fear of uncertainty, to that great encompassing mystery of life that is God.[7]

---

7. Chittister, *Called to Question*, 9.

One of the people I interviewed for this book is reform-minded Auxiliary Bishop Emeritus Pat Power who has long argued for change and often been rapped over the knuckles for it.

> The reform needed by the Church today will involve much more than just 'tinkering around the edges'. Issues such as the authoritarian nature of the Church, compulsory celibacy for the clergy, the participation of women in the Church, the teaching on sexuality in all aspects cannot be brushed aside. Listening must be a key component of reform and at times that will involve listening to unpalatable truths. It needs to be recognised that all wisdom does not reside exclusively in the present all male leadership of the Church and that the voices of the faithful must be heard.[8]

Some will agree with him and others not. Such is the challenge of reform. There will be builders, prophets, writers, artists, sociologists, laity, religious and priests who will contribute to it, and ideas will sometimes not mesh. There will be those who seek to hold onto remnants or dismantle them. This is part of the tension. Yet, the time seems right to take up the challenge.

In the final weeks of gathering together the threads of this book, I attended a meeting in Canberra of a significant group that has emerged in recent times—a group of people who identify as Catholic, but who have deep and enduring questions about the future of the Church.

At this forum, Francis Sullivan, the CEO of the Church's Truth, Justice and Healing Council spoke with emotion about the failures of the Church to address the problem of sexual abuse.

Every word he said was grounded in painstaking research and commitment to survivors.

When commissioned by the Church to undertake this role five years ago, Francis Sullivan's commitment to those who had been abused only grew, and throughout the duration of this role he has often drawn the ire of senior people in the institution.

At the end of the forum, he was asked a question about why he stays, a question many ask him. He said, plainly, without emotion:

---

8. Patrick Power, *Joy and Hope: Pilgrim, Priest and Bishop* (Melbourne: David Lovell Publishing, 2016).

'I'm staying . . . because I've got nowhere else to go.' Despite all the experiences he has had, all the testimonies he has heard of those who have suffered cruel abuse, he still wants to be part of the solution.

Not everyone will come to that conclusion, and it was clear that evening that some had left in despair and felt that being part of the institution, even to mend it, was beyond comprehension.

My survey respondents had much to say on what needs to change, and what needs to be reformed. Here's an example:

1. *I would analyse the culture of clericalism and try to persuade priests and bishops the re-examine the example of Christ to 'serve not to be served'*
2. *I would engage consultants in Time and Motion studies and work out where the priests and bishops should put in the most effort to make the church more in line with the person of Christ*
3. *I would make it mandatory for priests to update their training on a regular basis and make part of that training on the lines of management, because every parish or organisation is a mini business and should be handled as such*
4. *I would make the diocesan offices responsible for staffing of parishes and other organisations.*

It is important to address these ideas and suggestions.

Top-down hierarchical structures seem to be working less and less for people in the pews, at least in this country.

Some feel that being Catholic today comprises a life of suffering in an institution that is more and more irrelevant, disconnected and remote, and which does not listen to our cries.

There's much more to say. One might still argue, even after reading this short reflection, that there are still more reasons to leave the Church than to stay. Some may not align with those whose views I have quoted and may prefer another approach. Such is the breadth of the universal tradition. I believe there is space for all of us, strugglers and stragglers, saints and sinners, soldiers and sojourners.

I'm clearly not the only person who has asked these questions. As I researched, I found significant numbers of books about this subject—some with extremely similar names.

There is: *What Is The Point of Being Christian?* by Fr Timothy Radcliffe OP; *Why I Am a Catholic* by Garry Wills; *Why I Am a Catholic (and You Should Be Too)* by Brandon Vogt; *Why Be Catholic?* by Patrick Madrid, and then another book of the same name by William O'Malley SJ. There is *Why Stay Catholic?* by Michael Leach, and there are the testimonies of younger Catholics and older Catholics; lapsed Catholics and daily communicants.

I was contacted by a member of the parish I grew up in, a man with a doctorate in sociology, who had come across my survey via email. His name is Anthony Hogan.

Just a year ago, he had published his own text, a far more sociological and academic argument for reform than mine, entitled *Can We Start Again, Please?*

One of the most stunning books I read came to me unexpectedly.

A friend, who happens to be a parish priest, was speaking to me about the *Camino* to Santiago de Compostela and about a book he had read on the subject. He shared with me something of his homily on the subject.

He had quoted Australian actress and writer Ailsa Piper, who had written the book *Sinning across Spain* in 2012. As my friend described the book to me, he was checking the Spanish that he had clumsily shared with his congregation.

'*Duro, pero hermoso.*' 'Hard, but beautiful.'

This was how Piper had described her experience of the *Camino*, and it seemed to me to be an image of Church, too.

'*Camino*' means 'way' or 'journey', and in many ways, Catholicism is a faith of journeys/pilgrimage.

In a 3-year cycle at the mass, we go through each page of the Bible, the highs and lows, the peaks and valleys, the *chiaroscuro* of our Holy Book.

In the liturgical life, we live this, too: Christmas, Holy Week. We go through Holy Thursday and Good Friday, and finally arrive at Easter Sunday. We plod through Ordinary Time and perhaps feel the movement of the Spirit during Pentecost.

Straight after the conversation with my friend, I downloaded Piper's audiobook and listened to it, enthralled. As I listened, a social media post from an Australian Catholic publisher alerted me to another book by Piper, one she had written after forming an unlikely friendship with Monsignor Tony Doherty of Sydney.

I downloaded that book, too, and found myself falling in love with both real-life characters.

Towards the end of the book, *Attachments: Letters from a Most Unlikely Friendship*, Piper writes a letter to Doherty where she is trying to make sense of the Church, particularly considering the sexual abuse scandals, and she is particularly grappling with the teaching on human sexuality in the light of this.

In her letter to Doherty, she refers to the Church as a 'bullying father', referring to her own experience and perception of Church rules and teachings. Doherty expresses his hurt and surprise, and writes the most beautiful response:

> It's a curious thing: a frequent image of the church that comes to mind for me is that of a frail, aged mother grown old with her faults and limitations, her superstitions and rock like prejudices but one who has given life to me and who I love with a passion. If I'm honest with you, reading your words hurts. It hurts and renders me quite inadequate to answer you with truth and in words that would genuinely help you to appreciate the subtleties needing to be faced working in an institution like this. Your anger is not new to me . . . It outs into language the feelings of many in this seriously fractured time, about the serious blindness of those of us who identify with the Catholic Church . . . To describe this gigantic network of good and bad, fragile and strong, arrogant and unsure, self-satisfied and battlers as a bullying father is a little disconcerting. One of the colourful Gospel images is of a large net of odd fish, pulled up on a beach. I prefer that. We're a pretty mixed lot you know. If I am passionately committed to one thing is to explain to you how difficult it is to wrestle with the ambiguities and tensions within the church today, while at the same time holding onto integrity and be a genuine minister of the Gospel.[9]

There is something about a shared heritage in the Catholic tradition that often keeps us going.

Doherty's reflection is much better articulated than perhaps most of us who stay in the tension of this Church could muster—but certain images and metaphors help.

---

9. Ailsa Piper and Tony Doherty, *Attachments: Letters from a Most Unlikely Friendship* (Sydney: Allen and Unwin, 2017).

As mentioned earlier, in May 2019, a young spiritual seeker and Christian author Rachel Held Evans died suddenly of a serious infection.

She left behind a husband and two young children, as well as four incredible books about her experiences of growing up in an evangelical church and grappling with its teachings. In a blog, Evans talks of reform, of finding beauty in broken things:

> I've been thinking that this idea of learning a new skill so you can turn something ugly into something beautiful might be a good Lenten practice. Whether it's turning an AK-47 into a rake, an old tire into a flowerbed, or trash into a work of art, there is something profoundly fitting about struggling through the creative process with the goal of finishing something new by Easter to provide a tangible, hands-on experience in discipline, resurrection, and restoration.[10]

I read this blog after having been referred to it by a friend who had followed Evans' advice and taken up a new form of art.

In Japan, there is a type of pottery called *Kintsugi* or *Kintsukuroi* (Golden Mend). This stunning art form is the Japanese process of mending broken pottery using lacquer resin laced with gold or silver.

Basically, broken ceramics get given little spider-webbed/lacy threads of gold through them and are considered more beautiful than the original. Kintsukuroi has a deeper philosophical significance.

To me, this is a beautiful analogy for the Church, the idea that the broken pieces can be put back together and turned into something far more nuanced and beautiful.

Just like the broken body of Christ became the salvation of the world, there is a sense that through the cracks, the light, or indeed the gold, can shine through. You can interpret the brokenness in whatever way helps you make sense of it. To me, the brokenness is the tragic betrayal through abuse and the continued abuse by those who refused to believe or help the little ones.

---

10. Rachel Held Evans, 'Swords into Plowshares and Hate Mail into Origami', in *Rachel Held Evans* at <https://rachelheldevans.com/blog/origami-hate-mail?fbclid=IwAR2Bla7OHdxNoWaBy-EUUVnfsvS9_cPz3BFhJfbZqmuYcrlgyO4TrbIg6OM>. Accessed 6 September 2019.

Chris Lowney, a former Jesuit who works in corporate America wrote a book in 2017 called *Everyone Leads: How To Revitalise the Catholic Church*. In it he says:

> The Church is like any large corporation in one respect. In its early days, either the early church or the early years of Microsoft, you see all kinds of creativity, innovation, invention, people have nothing to lose, they're trying to find what works. Then you wake up and you're a vast enterprise, and it's very hard, when you have all kinds of buildings and structures and hierarchy and so on, to hang on to these very creative impulses that helped you get your great success in the first place. As a church we're going to have to figure a way out from under this.[11]

And so, the way forward and blueprint for change is not a neat little package. The answers to the question 'where can we find the truth, beauty and goodness of this tradition?' can perhaps only be found through deep contemplation, prayer, experience and, of course, through suffering. Some will find no answers. For some, the wounds are so deep, they will only be opened again and again.

I believe that there is a special place in heaven for those who have been abused in the Church, and the only God I want to know is one who will wipe away every tear from their eyes. The healing for many of those people will only come beyond the grave.

So, what does this mean for the Church in Australia? What does this mean for those of us who are clutching on by a thin, broken thread? How can the Church, and we—the body of Christ in this place—become a balm of mercy to those open wounds, particularly those wounds of abuse and cover-up, of ignorance and of bullying?

The answers have not come to me in this journey of writing in one fell swoop.

Sometimes, I light a candle and there still seems to be darkness.

Yet, the natural world often gives us moments of grace that remind us of God's presence, both in the light and the darkness.

Blythe Fike, an American writer for the website *Blessed Is She*, wrote in a reflection in 2019 of her gratitude for these signs:

---

11. Chris Lowney, *Everyone Leads: How To Revitalize the Catholic Church* (Lanham, Md: Rowman & Littlefield, 2017).

I'm always grateful for the real expression of grace extended to us through the natural world. The ebb and flow of dark to light and heat to cold; it's cyclical in a sometimes achingly painful way. We're not often ready for it, or we feel like the season ahead was just here. I think sometimes our liturgical life can feel a bit similar—Lent again, a little bit of penitential darkness . . . again. But then, without fail, comes the Light. It warms us at the core and radiates out, beyond us even and to the world.[12]

---

12. Fike, Blythe, 'The Spring Will Come', *Blessed Is She* at <https://blessedisshe.net/devotion/the-spring-will-come>. Accessed 9 September 2019.

Chapter Twelve
Jesus, Yesterday, Today and Tomorrow

The Gospel is absurd and the life of Jesus is meaningless unless we believe that He lived, died, and rose again with but one purpose in mind: to make brand-new creation. Not to make people with better morals but to create a community of prophets and professional lovers, men and women who would surrender to the mystery of the fire of the Spirit that burns within, who would live in ever greater fidelity to the omnipresent Word of God, who would enter into the centre of it all, the very heart and mystery of Christ, into the centre of the flame that consumes, purifies, and sets everything aglow with peace, joy, boldness, and extravagant, furious love. This, my friend, is what it really means to be a Christian.[1]

When I make time to pray, and I admit it's not nearly as frequent as it should be, I find it helpful to hold onto a cross.

I remember one cross that I gifted to a lady while on retreat, but up until that moment, it had been with me everywhere I went between 2005 and 2012.

On this particular cross, the figure of Jesus is a beautiful one, although it's not a traditional depiction. It was carved in great detail, with short hair and an Asian face.

Possibly, it was carved by a survivor of a landmine accident, or perhaps a Cambodian young adult who had suffered from polio in childhood and was left with a disability.

---

1. Brennan Manning, *The Furious Longing of God* (Colorado Springs: David C Cook, 2009), 125.

The cross comes from a workshop called Banteay Prieb, the House of the Dove, located about fifty kilometres from Phnom Penh, Cambodia's capital.

Banteay Prieb is a Gospel place. It echoes with the sorrow of the land which was soaked in blood and bone. The skulls of thousands who perished at the hands of the Khmer Rouge are housed there, and Banteay Prieb itself is near the site of a former Killing Field.

The place has both a darkness and a redemptive light about it.

Receiving the Eucharist in this place is tangible and moving. You cannot help but enter into the mystery of the broken body.

Cambodia has one of the highest percentages of anti-personnel mines in the world, second only to Sierra Leone.

It's estimated that there is more than one landmine for each member of the population (around thirteen million). As such, Cambodia has been at the forefront of the International Campaign to Ban Landmines.

At Banteay Prieb, the Jesuits and their associates have responded to this by training people with varied disabilities (some caused by landmines, and some by birth defects) in transferrable skills, such as sewing, woodwork, metal work and farming.

It was here that I first really understood the idea of the bread of life, and service of the poor.

It was here that I first met people who had struggled to feed their families, who ate rice for every meal, who lived a subsistence lifestyle.

The cross with a one-legged Jesus is one of Banteay Prieb's most famous symbols, and it comes in a wide variety of sizes. Some are carved out of wood, displaying an Asian face like the one I used to pray with.

The missing leg symbolises the loss of limbs due to landmine accidents and is positioned in such a way to communicate a broken, wounded Jesus.

Others are made from metal, welded into the shape of a cross with arms outstretched, again with two legs, one which is maimed.

The person of Jesus Christ is the main reason that most of my survey respondents have remained in the Church. For those who no longer attend, it's not because they have given up on Jesus, but for many there is a belief and sense that they no longer experience his presence in the Church. This sentiment is easy to understand.

For some, Jesus is the only reason they can fathom staying.

One priest, a former journalist with a passion for the poor who is gently and constructively critical of the institutional Church, answered the question: 'How do you remain a member of this tradition?' with the following:

> Jesus. Jesus is my north, my south, my east and my west. Obviously, it's my relationship with Christ [that] is the foundation, but it's the people, the people who keep me going. That's why I'm ordained. They decide whether I should be a priest.

It's usually during the sacraments that I am most likely to think about the person of Jesus, and because of this, I take them seriously.

In a particularly anxious time of my life, I clung scrupulously to the sacraments, trying to stay close.

Sitting in church after Reconciliation, I was struck by the two sides of God, human and divine. The divinity of God is such an out of reach concept for me. I don't feel I have the capacity to understand it and when I try, it remains just beyond where I am.

Looking up at the cross though, I feel his humanity. I am awed that God gave his son, to become human, to enter our world and live among us, humble flawed people.

I am struck by the physicality of Jesus. How did he feel at the Last Supper when he knew that one of his friends would betray him? How did he deal with the knowledge that Peter, his rock, would deny he ever knew him, not once but three times? The betrayal must have been heart-wrenching and yet he forgave them.

In the garden of Gethsemane, Jesus took three disciples and said to them: 'My soul is overwhelmed with sorrow to the point of death. Stay here and keep watch with me.' He prayed three times to God, scared and alone as his disciples failed three times to remain awake.

How did it feel to be mocked and ridiculed? I can't imagine how much the whip smarted on his back, how the crown of thorns stung and how heavy the cross was, borne under all those hurts. The thought of the nails makes my hands and feet curl.

God surely knew that his divinity and his unconditional love was a challenge for us to comprehend. So, he made his son human so that he could walk among us, feeling human emotion and pain. Although Jesus is the most perfect human who ever lived, his presence and his life was the most relatable way God could communicate with us.

Even though he was without sin, we see in the Bible that Jesus faced challenges, was hurt by betrayal, got angry, felt joy, was part of a human family, and felt pain.

I am in awe of the sacrifice God made in creating Jesus in human form, and then giving him up on the cross so that we might glimpse that divinity and understand the depth of his love for us.

Given that the Church in Australia is somewhat 'on the nose', it can be difficult socially at times when one still identifies as Catholic, even amongst close friends and family.

Throw into the mix the name of Jesus and, often, it's as though you have grown an extra head. Awkward silence. The landscape changes completely.

Reclaiming the name of Jesus, and a sense of wonder has to be part of the renewal of the Church. Jesus' life, human and divine, needs to be the roadmap, the *Camino*, the pilgrimage that informs us. It will likely mean the cross, but at times there will be glimpses of the resurrection.

Author Brennan Manning wrote that while we fall again and again in our sinful nature, we live in imitation of Christ when we are able.

How to do this? Perhaps through some of the ways and means proposed in this short text.

> The greatest single cause of atheism in the world today is Christians: who acknowledge Jesus with their lips, walk out the door, and deny Him by their lifestyle. That is what an unbelieving world simply finds unbelievable.[2]

In many ways, the more we learn about institutional faith, the less Christian we become. It has not been lost on me during this project how strident we can become about our petty church battles, and how little these really have to do with the Gospel of Jesus. At the crux of it, our Church simply must return to its roots, its foundations, to the person of Jesus Christ.

---

2. Attributed to Brennan Manning, author of *The Ragamuffin Gospel* and *The Furious Longing of God*.

Epilogue

Tribes are an interesting thing. They can exclude and include, give meaning and strip people of their individuality.

They can bind people together and separate them out, carefully sorting the sheep from the goats.

Tribe Catholic is one of the biggest tribes. It is a diverse one, and as its name suggests, a universal one.

It is a tribe that I am at once proud and privileged to be part of, while at times feeling deeply apologetic and ashamed.

Its grip on my life is all-encompassing. It has accompanied me from when I was but 'a twinkle in my father's eye', and on into birth and baptism. It has been a source of communion, fracture, relationship, reconciliation, confirmation. It has heralded moments of desolation and consolation that are tattooed on my soul.

Whether breathing in the heady fumes of incense at a high cathedral mass, or smelling soup wafting from the Vinnies van on a cold winter night, it is there.

Whether singing 'Alleluia, the Lord is Risen', or sitting in a Garden of Gethsemane with the words, 'My God, why have you abandoned me?', there remains for me a deep, sonorous sense that the current crises in the Church can indeed be overcome, if only we start again each day, perhaps with a morning offering or simply the Jesus Prayer: Lord, Jesus Christ, son of the living God, have mercy on me, a sinner.[1]

---

1. 'The Jesus Prayer', *Our Catholic Prayers* at https://www.ourcatholicprayers.com/jesus-prayer.html. Accessed 17 October 2019.

This story, in many ways, begins and ends with cups of tea, coffee and bucket loads of conversation. The dialogue has been broad and often fraught.

Some conversations have left me with a heavy heart and others with a lightness in my step.

In reflecting recently on my journey of faith, I thought back to a time some years ago when I was less cynical about the hierarchical machinations in the Vatican.

I was able to think well of the men in the pointy hats, and while more worldly wise about some of the politics involved, generally, I still do. Now, I see them as human, trapped, like myself in a world that often has trouble distinguishing fantasy from reality.

It was 2013 and the conclave that would elect Francis had not yet begun. I held a conclave party at my apartment and made a conclave pizza. On it were lots of little cherry tomatoes to represent the zucchettos of the cardinals and one piece of bocconcini cheese to represent the white hat of the Pope.

Earlier, in the lively social media commentary around #conclave2013, a meme emerged in Spanish with a cartoon of a grumpy looking cardinal with a thought bubble. In this image the window to the Sistine Chapel is closed and the thought bubble reads: 'Twitter will be completely prohibited from the conclave.' Outside the window is a frantic dove, knocking on the glass. 'Let me in', says the dove, 'I'm not twitter, I'm the Holy Spirit.'[2]

Well, it does seem that the Holy Spirit managed to make its way into the Sistine Chapel in 2013.

Some might even go as far as to say that the joy of the Gospel seems to be re-entering the Church, or at the very least, Pope Francis is calling people back to basics and modelling beauty in simplicity.

He uses humour; indeed, he is rarely seen in public without a warm smile. He is open about his frailty and is quick to admit when he is found to have spoken in error.

The anecdotes and stories throughout this text, and indeed centuries of similar ones, are what I want to be part of.

My sisters and brothers in faith who choose to stay with me will experience the peaks and troughs, the ups and downs, the swings and roundabouts.

---

2. Edizz, Soy el Espíritu Santo! (I am the Holy Spirit!), Humor Gráfico at https://www.humor-grafico.com/tag/espiritu/. Accessed 17 October 2019.

As the Book of Ecclesiastes says, 'there is a time for every purpose under heaven'. (Eccl 3:1)
We will weep and we will laugh.
The beautiful St Louis Jesuit hymn by Bob Dufford 'Be Not Afraid' paraphrases this in its final stirring verse:

> Blessed are your poor,
> For the kingdom shall be theirs.
> Blessed are you that weep and mourn,
> For one day you shall laugh.
> And if wicked men insult and hate you
> All because of me
> Blessed, blessed are you[3]

I am choosing to be blessed, and to bless the Lord at all times.
I choose to bless the mess.
I choose to find beauty in the brokenness, in the ashes.
I'm choosing the 'chiaroscuro', the light and shade, and sometimes the darkness.
Former Anglican priest and writer Barbara Brown Taylor has a captivating phrase in her book *Learning to walk in the dark*:
'...new life starts in the dark. Whether it is a seed in the ground, a baby in the womb, or Jesus in the tomb, it starts in the dark.'[4]
It is nearing the end of 2019 and the Catholic Church is in the news headlines again, prompting all manner of dinner table discussions and commentary.
On social media, the commentary can be unfiltered, unmoderated, unregulated, and often unkind. The dialogue with those people who take it upon themselves to be self-proclaimed guardians of orthodoxy at the expense of pastoral sensibility can be tricky. No doubt well-meaning keyboard warriors spill forth bile, naming and shaming anyone who might appear to have a tinge of sympathy for those at the margins. No one escapes the ire, not even, or perhaps especially, Pope Francis.

---

3. Bob Dufford, 'Be Not Afraid', *Catholic Hymn* at http://catholichymn.blogspot.com/2015/10/be-not-afraid.html. Accessed 17 October 2019.
4. Barbara Brown Taylor, *Learning to Walk in the Dark* (New York: Harper One, 2014), 129.

Everyone has an opinion, and it seems that this is because people care deeply.

Cardinal George Pell remains in jail for historical child sexual offences, and at the time of writing, is appealing to the High Court for one final opportunity to clear his name.

The Pope is holding a Synod to look at evangelisation in the Amazon region that will discuss many of the issues that have been on the minds of Catholics for fifty years or more—questions such as optional celibacy for the clergy, ordination of women to the diaconate, and what to do when there are no longer people to facilitate the sacraments.

Religious women have launched their own #MeToo movement in response to sexual abuse by priests, and French journalist Frederic Martel has expended four years and 700 pages on homosexuality in the Roman Curia and hypocrisy at the highest level of the Church.

Some laud Francis for his progressive views and vision for change, and others, even curial officials, demonise him to the point of caricature.

This year, both the macro and micro level of church involvement have been in sharp focus.

I have sat in parishes with just a few people, and later in the same week witnessed the spectacle of an energetic youth festival with thousands of young people singing praise and worship anthems. I witnessed an extraordinary moment where a crowd of 400 people spontaneously dropped to their knees as a priest walked around with a monstrance displaying the blessed sacrament.

I have attended forums of angry people who are tired and despairing that change will happen, while just days earlier I had watched a bishop berating families at a confirmation mass for not knowing when to sit and stand.

I have sat down for a cup of tea with divorced, single, cohabiting and lapsed Catholics, and given my black lace mantilla to an 18-year-old student who has developed a love for the Latin Mass.

I have seen the positivity of youth ministers in parishes and schools who have not yet become jaded with the institution, and commiserated with octogenarian theologians who are hanging on by a thread.

The harvest is ripe for change. There are windows of change that are being opened, and doors that seem to remain locked.

The cycle continues. There is a time to be born and a time to die, a time to sow and a time to reap.

We are baptised with water and blessed with oils.

We feast on the bread of angels even when we do not feel worthy, and even question the worthiness of the one who consecrates that bread.

We confess our sins, even when it is unclear how much longer the seal of sanctity will remain.

We sit in the parish and still see young people choosing the name of a saint and being confirmed, receiving the Holy Spirit.

We participate in councils and work in Catholic organisations.

We attend mass in parishes where both priest and music ministry have lost their mojo.

We write submissions to inquiries and commissions, hoping that our pens may be mighty enough to make a difference.

This faith is not for the faint-hearted, but it is one that, in its purest and best form, is the most important community we will ever belong to.

The harvest is plenty and the labourers are few.

I can only conlude with a call to hope. While much rightly gives rise to despair, frustration, anger, and for some a sense of betrayal that simply cannot be overcome, I wish to be a part of the rebuilding effort.

'Go rebuild my house, the Lord said to St Francis of Assisi.[5]

How literally Francis took this command; he picked up his hammer.

Almost a millennium later the Bishop of Rome took the name Francis and opened up conversations that seemed frozen in time during previous pontificates.

We need to take up the proverbial hammer, and perhaps a sickle too. More importantly though, we need to lay some foundations, build our house on solid rock.

Whatever of our scales we need to shed as a Church in order to be renewed, it will need courage and vision.

There remains a seed of hope in my heart; a sense that, if I leave, more will be lost than gained.

---

5. Regis J Armstrong and William J Short and J A Wayne Hellmann, *Francis of Assisi: Early Documents, Volume 2, The Founder* (New York: New City Press, 2000), 249.

My hope is no longer, perhaps never was, in the institutional church, but in the basic, daily acts that make up a life of faith.

A sign of the cross as prayer comes on over the loud speaker at the school where I teach; a short verse read from the bible after a long day, a verse that is ever ancient and ever new, and speaks into the moment, even though it was written just a few years after Jesus' death.

In many ways, the more we learn about institutional faith, the less Christian we become. It has not been lost on me during this project how strident we can become about our petty church battles, and how little these really have to do with the Gospel of Jesus.

Once we have studied theology and know the words to the '*Tantum ergo*' ('Only therefore') and have had a run in with a tribunal, perhaps we realise that these things lead us to know less about the carpenter from Nazareth.

I honestly believe I was a better Christian when I did not know what a ciborium, a cincture, or a cilice were.

It is likely that in my lifetime, women in the church will not wear a surplice, a soutane or a stole.

Monstrances, magisterium, and mysticism all have their place, but most Catholics will spend most of their lives without a clue as to what they even are. At best, they might understand they are simply a vessel, big words and experiences that cannot be named or understood.

By simplifying, breaking down, and starting from scratch, it is possible we might discover beauty in simplicity.

It is possible that parables and the paraclete and the paschal mystery might be enough for us to start again, because here we have the way, the spirit and the reason for our faith.

Sometimes my stomach drops when it's time to attend yet another uninspiring mass, and it drops further when I realise that attending is often an act of defiance against my conscience, a conscience that holds the stories of so much hurt via this Church.

Pithy answers and silver bullets will not be enough to restore for some what has been lost. It is my fear that for some, this book and these reflections will be simply that: too little, too late.

A dear priest friend quipped: 'There are lots of people here who will tell you that Jesus is the answer, but what I want to know is: what is the question?'

I suspect that the challenge is that the answers and even the questions will be different for each of us. Paul's letter to the Corinthians endures today: 'We are one body but many parts' (1 Cor 12:12).

There are problems to be solved, and light that may not penetrate our souls until we meet God face-to-face in heaven.

And yet, my friends, I want to be part of a solution, a reformation, a rebuilding. I don't want to stand idly by, throw in the towel, or let the forces of evil win.

I want to sit down in community and assemble the pieces.

I want to be the one who stops on the roadside and applies oil to the wounds of the stranger and wraps them again and again in clean, fresh cloths.

I want to pour myself out in service and fight belligerently and without ceasing for justice until I run out of breath.

I want to sit at the foot of the cross with my head bowed down and listen to the cries of those who have been crucified with Christ; those abused, betrayed, ignored.

I want to anoint the feet of those in need with jars of ointment. I want to sit in prayer with the small, the broken, the scarred, the wounded, the anxious and the poor.

I want to apply the balm of mercy, sing the songs of the ages, eat the bread of the broken body, and piece by piece, rebuild this reign of God as much as possible on the earth.

The way, I think, to begin this rebuilding process is by looking back, and looking forward.

As I finish this writing journey, I am reminded of the words of poet James McAuley's 'In a late hour'.

Once again, it is by gathering together fragments, words and thoughts of the wide, expansive communion that is the Catholic Church that gives me the impetus, energy and hope to start again.

In the poem, McAuley writes:

> While the stars run distracted
> And from wounds deep rancours flow
> While the mystery is enacted
> I will not let you go.[6]

---

6. James McAuley, 'In a Late Hour', *Australian Poetry Library* at <https://www.poetrylibrary.edu.au/poets/mcauley-james/poems/in-a-late-hour-0151074>. Accessed 17 October 2019.

References

@Archbishop Mark (Mark Coleridge), 'Reflecting on joy with thousands of young people at #ACYF17. . .' 8 December 2017, 5:31pm at <https://twitter.com/ArchbishopMark/status/939019500422230016>. Accessed 8 December 2017.

@audreyassad, 'It's really starting to hit home to me that many Christians see the church more as a country club than a hospital. . .'

ACBC Pastoral Research Office, *Building Stronger Parishes* at <https://www.buildingstrongerparishes.catholic.org.au/>. Accessed 9 September 2019.

America Media, *Jesuitical* at <https://www.americamagazine.org/jesuitical>. Accessed 9 September 2019.

Assad, Audrey, 'Even unto Death', in *Inheritance* [CD] (n.p.: Fortunate Fall Records, 2016).

Australia. Royal Commission into Institutional Responses to Child Sexual Abuse, 'Religious Institutions', *Royal Commission into Institutional Responses to Child Sexual Abuse: Religious Institutions* at <https://www.childabuseroyalcommission.gov.au/religious-institutions>. Accessed 9 September 2019.

Bernardin, Joseph and Thomas Nairn, *The Seamless Garment: Writings on the Consistent Ethic of Life* (Maryknoll, NY: Orbis Books, 2008).

Bessey, Sarah, *Jesus Feminist: An Invitation to Revisit the Bible's View of Women: Exploring God's Radical Notion That Women Are People, Too* (Nashville: Howard Books, 2013).

Câmara, Dom Helder, and Francis McDonagh, *Dom Helder Camara*. (Maryknoll, N.Y.: Orbis Books, 2009).

Chesterton, Gilbert Keith, and Aidan Mackey, *The Collected Works of GK Chesterton: [vol]. X; Collected Poetry Part 1* (San Francisco: Ignatius, 1994).

Chittister, Joan, *Called to Question: A Spiritual Memoir* (Lanham, Md: Sheed & Ward, 2009).

Chmiel, Mark, *The Book of Mev* (New York: Xlibris, 2006).

Claiborne, Shane, *The Irresistible Revolution: Living as an Ordinary Radical* (Grand Rapids, Michigan: Zondervan, 2006).

Corson, G. (2019). *OSV: Our Sunday Visitor Weekly*. Retrieved from https://www.osv.com/TheChurch/Article/TabId/563/ArtMID/13751/ArticleID/9934/Top-Ten-reasons-to-send-your-children-to-Catholic-Schools.aspx

Day, Dorothy, *The Long Loneliness: The Autobiography of D. Day* (Garden City, N.Y.: Doubleday & Co, 1959).

Day, Thomas, *Why Catholics Can't Sing: The Culture of Catholicism and the Triumph of Bad Taste*. (New York: Crossroad, 1990).

Ellsberg, Robert, *Blessed among All Women*: *Women, Saints, Prophets, and Witnesses for Our Time* (London: Darton Longman & Todd, 2006).

Evans, Rachel Held, *A Year of Biblical Womanhood: How a Liberated Woman Found Herself Sitting on Her Roof, Covering Her Head, and Calling Her Husband 'Master'* (Nashville: Thomas Nelson, 2012).

Evans, Rachel Held, *Searching for Sunday: Loving, Leaving, and Finding the Church* (Nashville: Thomas Nelson, 2015).

Evans, Rachel Held, 'Swords into Plowshares and Hate Mail into Origami', *Rachel Held Evans* at <https://rachelheldevans.com/blog/origami-hate-mail?fbclid=IwAR2Bla7OHdxNoWaBy-EUUVnfsvS9_cPz3BFhJf-bZqmuYcrlgyO4TrbIg6OM>. Accessed 6 September 2019.

Fike, Blythe, 'The Spring Will Come', *Blessed Is She* at <https://blessedisshe.net/devotion/the-spring-will-come>. Accessed 9 September 2019.

Getty, Keith, and Kristyn Getty, *Sing! How Worship Transforms Your Life, Family, and Church* (Nashville: B & H Publishing, 2017).

Greeley, Andrew, *The Catholic Imagination* (Berkeley, Calif: University of California Press, 2001).

Harrison Warren, Tish, *Liturgy of the Ordinary: Sacred Practices in Everyday Life* (Downers Grove, Ill.: IVP Books, 2016).

Hennessy, Kate, *Dorothy Day: The World Will Be Saved by Beauty* (New York: Scribner, 2017).

Hogan, Anthony, *Can We Start Again, Please? Towards Reform of the Catholic Church* (Canberra: The Author, 2018).

Ignatius, of Loyola, Saint and Joseph Tylenda, *A Pilgrim's Journey: The Autobiography of Ignatius of Loyola* (Revised edition) (San Francisco: Ignatius Press, 2001).

Ignatius, of Loyola, Saint and Thomas Corbishley, *The Spiritual Exercises of Saint Ignatius of Loyola* (Mineola, NY: Dover Publications, 2011).

Leach, Michael, *Why Stay Catholic? Unexpected Answers to a Life-Changing Question* (Chicago: Loyola Press, 2011).

Leonard, Richard, *Hatch, Match and Dispatch: A Catholic Guide to Sacraments* (New York: Paulist Press, 2019).

Leonard, Richard, *Why Bother Praying?* (New York: Paulist Press, 2013).

Lernoux, Penny, *People of God: The Struggle for World Catholicism* (New York: Viking, 1989).

Lowney, Chris, *Everyone Leads: How To Revitalize the Catholic Church* (Lanham, Md: Rowman & Littlefield, 2017).

Madrid, Patrick, *Why Be Catholic?* (New York: Image, 2014).

Manning, Brennan, *The Furious Longing of God* (Colorado Springs: David C. Cook, 2009).

Martin, James, *Becoming Who You Are: Insights on the True Self from Thomas Merton and Other Saints* (Mahwah, NJ: HiddenSpring, 2006).

Martin, James, *Jesus: A Pilgrimage* (New York: Harper One, 2014).

McGrath, John, 'Possibilities for New Evangelisation of Catholic School Students, Teachers and Parents', in *Journal of Religious Education*. 62 (2014): 15–24 at <https://doi.org/10.1007/s40839-014-0002-5>. Accessed 9 September 2019.

Millard, Bart, *I Can Only Imagine* (Santa Monica, Lionsgate, 2018).

Millard, Bart and Mercy Me, 'I Can Only Imagine', in *The Worship Project* (USA: Mercy Me, 1999).

Moltmann, Jürgen, *The Crucified God: The Cross of Christ as the Foundation and Criticism of Christian Theology*, 40th anniversary edition (Minneapolis: Fortress, 2015).

Morris, William Martin, *Benedict XVI and Me and the Cardinals Three* (Adelaide: ATF Press, 2014).

Niequist, Shauna, *Bread & Wine: A Love Letter to Life around the Table, with Recipes* (Grand Rapids, Mich: Zondervan, 2013).

O'Malley, William, *Why Be Catholic?* (New York: Crossroad, 1993).

O'Donohue, John, *Beauty: The Invisible Embrace* (New York: HarperCollins Publishers, 2004).

Piper, Ailsa. *Sinning across Spain: Walking the Camino* Updated edition (Melbourne: Melbourne University Press, 2017).

Piper, Ailsa, and Tony Doherty, *Attachments: Letters from a Most Unlikely Friendship*. (Sydney: Allen and Unwin, 2017).

Pope Francis, *Chrism Mass: Homily, Saint Peter's Basilica (Holy Thursday, 28 March 2013)* at <http://w2.vatican.va/content/francesco/en/homilies/2013/documents/papa-francesco_20130328_messa-crismale.html>. Accessed 10 September 2019.

Pope Francis, interviewed by Antonio Spadaro, 'A Big Heart Open to God: An Interview with Pope Francis', *America*, 30 September 2013 at <https://www.americamagazine.org/faith/2013/09/30/big-heart-open-god-interview-pope-francis>. Accessed 9 September 2019.

Pope Francis, *Evangelii Gaudium: Apostolic Exhortation on the Proclamation of the Gospel in Today's World (24 November 2013)* at <http://w2.vatican.va/content/francesco/en/apost_exhortations/documents/papa-francesco_esortazione-ap_20131124_evangelii-gaudium.html>. Accessed 9 September 2019.

Pope Francis, interview with Andrea Tornielli, translated by Oonagh Stransky, *The Name of God Is Mercy: A Conversation with Andrea Tornielli* (London: Bluebird Books for Life, 2014).

Pope John Paul II, *Letter of His Holiness Pope John Paul II to Artists* at <https://w2.vatican.va/content/john-paul-ii/en/letters/1999/documents/hf_jp-ii_let_23041999_artists.html>. Accessed 9 September 2019.

Power, Patrick, *Joy and Hope: Pilgrim, Priest and Bishop* (Melbourne: David Lovell Publishing, 2016).

Prowse, Christopher, 'Homily: Chrism Mass 2018' at <http://cgcatholic.org.au/about/our-archbishop/homilies-teachings-pastoral-letters/homilies-2018/chrism-mass/>. Accessed 9 September 2019.

Puleo, Mev, *The Struggle Is One: Voices and Visions of Liberation* (Albany, NY: State University of New York Press, 1994).

Radcliffe, Timothy, *Why Go to Church?: The Drama of the Eucharist* (London: Continuum, 2009).

Radcliffe, Timothy, *What Is the Point of Being a Christian?* (London: Bloomsbury, 2013).

Research Management Group and Australian Catholic University and Australian Episcopal Conference and Australian Conference of Leaders of Religious Institutes and Bishops' Committee for Justice, Development and Peace, *Woman and Man: One in Christ Jesus: Report on the Participation of Women in the Catholic Church in Australia* (Sydney, NSW: HarperCollinsReligious, 1999).

Rolheiser, Ron, 'Kissing the Leper', *Ron Rolheiser, OMI* at http://ronrolheiser.com/kissing-the-leper/#.XQHsz4gzbIV. Accessed 9 September 2019.

Ryan, Maurice, and Patricia Malone, *Exploring the Religion Classroom: A Guidebook for Catholic Schools* (Wentworth Falls, NSW: Social Science Press, 1996).

Staudt, R Jared, 'Beauty Will Save the World: From the Mouth of an Idiot to the Pen of a Pope', *Crisis Magazine*, 10 July 2013 at <http://www.crisismagazine.com/2013/beauty-will-save-the-world-from-the-mouth-of-an-idiot-to-the-pen-of-a-pope>. Accessed 9 September 2019.

Sullivan, Francis, 'Where To from Here?', in *Catalyst for Renewal Incorporated* at <http://www.tjhcouncil.org.au/media/132927/170310-SPEECH-Catalyst-for-Renewal-Hunters-Hill-Francis-Sullivan.pdf>. Accessed 9 September 2019.

Teresa, Mother, and Brian Kolodiejchuk, *Come Be My Light: The Private Writings of the 'Saint of Calcutta'* (New York: Doubleday, 2007).

Thibodeaux, Mark, and Mark Link, *Armchair Mystic: Easing into Contemplative Prayer* (Cincinnati, Ohio: St Anthony Messenger Press, 2001).

Tolkien, John Ronald Reuel, *The Letters of JRR Tolkien* (Boston, Mariner Books, 2000).

United States Conference of Catholic Bishops and Catholic Church, *Sing To the Lord: Music in Divine Worship* (Washington, DC: United States Conference of Catholic Bishops, 2007).

Vatican Radio, 'Pope Comforts Pregnant Single Woman' at <http://www.archivioradiovaticana.va/storico/2013/09/13/pope_comforts_pregnant_single_woman/in2-728305>. Accessed 9 September 2019.

Vatican.va, *Musicam Sacram: Instruction on Music in the Liturgy*, 5 March 1967 at http://www.vatican.va/archive/hist_councils/ii_vatican_council/documents/vat-ii_instr_19670305_musicam-sacram_en.html. Accessed 9 September 2019.

Vogt, Brandon, *Why I Am Catholic (and You Should Be Too)* (Notre Dame, Ind: Ave Maria Press, 2017).

Voskamp, Ann, *One Thousand Gifts: A Dare To Live Fully Right Where You Are* (Grand Rapids, Mich: Zondervan, 2012).

Weber, Kerry, *Mercy in the City: How To Feed the Hungry, Give Drink To the Thirsty, Visit the Imprisoned, and Keep Your Day Job* (Chicago: Loyola Press, 2014).

Weigel, George, *The Courage To Be Catholic: Crisis, Reform and the Future of the Church* (New York: Basic Books, 2007).

White, Michael, and Tom Corcoran, *Rebuilt: The Story of a Catholic Parish: Awakening the Faithful, Reaching the Lost, Making Church Matter* (Notre Dame, Ind: Ave Maria Press, 2013).

Wills, Garry, *Why I Am a Catholic* (Boston: Houghton Mifflin Co, 2003).

Lightning Source UK Ltd.
Milton Keynes UK
UKHW010631270221
379429UK00002B/116